LEARNING THE
NEW BREVIARY

by

BERNARD A. HAUSMANN, S. J.

IMPRIMI POTEST

J. R. CONNERY, S. J.
Praepositus Provincialis
Provinciae Chicagiensis, S. J.
die 8 novembris, 1960.

NIHIL OBSTAT

J. J. BRENNAN, M.A.
Censor Deputatus

IMPRIMATUR

✠ FRANCIS CARDINAL SPELLMAN
Archbishop of New York
April 18, 1961

CONTENTS

PART I

THE DIVINE OFFICE: ITS NATURE AND PARTS

CHAPTER I

INTRODUCTION

I. THE NEW TERMINOLOGY

1. The Divine Office is an essential part of the liturgical day. The term *liturgical day* is defined in the rubrics as a day sanctified by liturgical actions, particularly by the Eucharistic Sacrifice and the public prayer of the Church, which is the Divine Office. Liturgical days are divided into four classes, which, in descending order of rank, are designated simply as days of the first (I), second (II), third (III), and fourth (IV) class. As you might suspect, a liturgical day of the first class is a day on which both Mass and Office are of a feast of the first class, or of a Sunday of the first class, or of a vigil or ferial of the first class. The same is true in due proportion of the other classes.

2. The Sundays of the year fall into only two classes. The Sundays of the first class are all the Sundays of Advent, the Sundays of Lent, Easter Sunday, Low Sunday, and Pentecost Sunday. All other Sundays are of the second class. The rank of a Sunday does not determine the nature of the Office recited, but the rank of the feast which can displace the Sunday Office. In general, no feast can displace a Sunday of the first class. Even a

feast of the second class, unless it be a feast of Our
Lord, cannot displace a Sunday of the second class. A
feast of the first class, however, always displaces a
Sunday of the second class.

3. The feasts of the ecclesiastical year are divided
into three classes and are designated as feasts of the first
(I) class, of the second (II) class, and of the third
(III) class. The class of a feast determines the nature
of the Office said in its celebration.

4. Three feasts, Christmas, Easter, and Pentecost,
have octaves. An octave is defined as the celebration of
a greater feast for eight continuous days. Octaves are
of two kinds: octaves of the first (I) class; namely,
those of Easter and Pentecost; and octaves of the second (II) class; namely, the octave of Christmas. All
days within octaves of the first class are liturgical days
of the first class. Days within an octave of the second
class are liturgical days of the second class; the octave
day, however, is of the first class.

5. A Vigil is defined as a liturgical day which precedes a feast and serves as a preparation for it. Vigils
are of three classes. Vigils of the I class are those of
Christmas and Pentecost. Those of the II class are the
vigils of the Ascension of Our Lord, of the Assumption
of the B.V.M., of the Nativity of St. John the Baptist,
and of the feast of Saints Peter and Paul Apostles.
There is only one vigil of the III class; it is the vigil of
St. Laurence.

6. The days of the week, all except Sunday, are
called ferial days. Thus, Monday is feria II (there is no
feria I), Tuesday is feria III, etc. However, Saturday
is never referred to as feria VII but always by its He-

brew name Sabbatum. There are four classes of ferial days. Those of the I class are Ash Wednesday and the ferial days of Holy Week. Those of the II class are the weekdays of Advent from the 17th to the 23rd of December; also the Ember Days of Advent, Lent, and September. Those of the III class are the days of Lent not yet mentioned and all the days of Advent to December 16th inclusively. All the other ferial days belong to the IV class.

II. THE ROMAN BREVIARY

7. The Roman Breviary is a liturgical book containing the Divine Office. If published in one volume, it is called a *totum*. More usually it is published in two volumes. They are officially designated as *Tomus Prior* and *Tomus Alter*. Whether published in one or two volumes, each volume contains the following essential parts: the *Ordinarium*, the *Psalterium*, the *Proprium de Tempore*, the *Proprium Sanctorum*, and the *Commune Sanctorum*. The *Ordinarium* contains an outline of the various hours of the Divine Office and those prayers which never vary from day to day. It corresponds, therefore, to the *Ordo Missæ* of the missal. The *Psalterium* contains the psalms for the various Hours for each day of the week. The *Proprium de Tempore* contains the variable parts for the Sunday Office and in addition three lessons for each day of the week. These lessons are taken from various books of the Bible and are called Scripture Occurring lessons. In the second volume of the breviary the lessons from a

Homily on the Gospel are not found with the other lessons for the Sunday, but in a section by itself at the end of the *Proprium de Tempore.* The *Proprium Sanctorum* contains those parts of the Office for the saints in the calendar of the universal Church which are proper to each saint. The *Commune Sanctorum* has almost complete Offices for the various classes of saints; namely, Apostles, Martyrs, Confessors, etc.

8. Besides these essential parts, other minor parts may also be found in each volume of the breviary. Among these are the *Officia propria diœceseos, nationis, vel ordinis* and many useful prayers and blessings. The section *Officia propria diœceseos,* as its name indicates, is nothing else than a supplement to the *Proprium Sanctorum* and contains Offices which are not common to the universal Church, but are celebrated in a particular diocese.

NOTE. To acquire familiarity with the content and divisions of the breviary, it is suggested that the student page through one of the volumes of the breviary. An hour or two thus spent will prove a profitable investment.

III. THE DIVINE OFFICE

9. The Divine Office consists of seven Canonical Hours, namely: Matins and Lauds (counted as one Hour), Prime, Terce, Sext, None, Vespers, and Compline. All who are bound to the recitation of the Divine Office must daily recite (vocally) these seven hours.

10. There are five classes of Offices. They are:

a) The *Officium dominicale,* or Sunday Office. This

is the Office which is said on Sundays. In the breviary it has a section practically to itself; namely, the *Proprium de Tempore.*

b) The *Officium festivum,* or festal Office. This is the Office which is said on feasts of the I class. Many of the parts of such Offices are proper to each feast and are printed in full in the *Proprium Sanctorum.* If not all are printed, references will be given there as to where the missing parts can be found.

c) The *Officium semifestivum,* or the semifestal Office. This is the Office for all feasts of the II class. Fewer parts of such Offices are proper to the Office. The proper parts are again found in the *Proprium Sanctorum.*

d) The *Officium ordinarium,* or ordinary Office. This is the Office for all feasts of the III class. The name probably derives from the fact that this Office is said more frequently than any other. The proper parts of this Office are again found in the *Proprium Sanctorum.*

e) The *Officium feriale,* or ferial Office. It is said on days when no feast of a saint occurs or when the feast of a saint may not be celebrated; for example, on Ash Wednesday. It is also said on vigils of the II and III class.

11. The rubrics with regard to the ceremonies of the Divine Office, when to make the sign of the cross, when to stand, genuflect, when to sit, are of obligation only when the Divine Office is said in choir or in common. The rubric, however, goes on to say that it is fitting for one saying the Office alone to keep the rubrics with regard to the sign of the cross.

12. The rules governing the sign of the cross in the recitation of the Divine Office are as follows: Make the large sign of the cross from forehead to breast, from left shoulder to right

a) At the beginning of each hour at the verse *Deus, in adiutorium.*

b) After the *lectio brevis* of Prime and Compline when reciting the verse *Adiutorium nostrum.*

c) When beginning the absolution *Indulgentiam* after the *Confiteor* in the Hour of Compline.

d) At the beginning of each of the three canticles *Benedictus, Magnificat,* and *Nunc dimittis.*

e) At the benediction at the end of Prime and of Compline.

f) At the verse *Divinum auxilium* at the end of the Office.

Make a sign of the cross on the lips at the beginning of Matins at the words. *Dombine, labia mea aperies.*

Make a sign of the cross on the breast in Compline at the words *Converte nos,* which occur shortly after the *Confiteor.*

13. The Proper Time for the Recitation of the Canonical Hours.—The new rubrics give as a purpose of the Canonical Hours the sanctification of the hours of the day. They point out that this purpose will be better achieved and the Canonical Hours recited with greater spiritual profit if they are recited at the times for which they were composed. Matins was intended for the night hours; Lauds for the very early morning; Prime, Terce, Sext, and None, as their names indicate, for the first, third, sixth, and ninth hours of the day; Vespers for the early evening; and Compline as the final prayer of the day.

However, the new rubrics still permit the anticipation of Matins. For any good reason it may be said, even in choir or in common, at any time after two o'clock in the afternoon of the preceding day. Lauds may no longer be anticipated.

The rubrics also state explicitly that anyone bound to the recitation of the Canonical Hours satisfies his obligation if he recites them at any time between midnight and midnight.

14. Indulgences Attached to the Divine Office.—

1) Clerics in Holy Orders, who devoutly recite the entire Divine Office, even when separated into parts, before the Blessed Sacrament whether exposed for public adoration or reserved in the tabernacle, are granted: A plenary indulgence, if they make their confession, receive Holy Communion and pray for the intentions of the Holy Father.

Those, however, who recite only a part of the Divine Office before the Blessed Sacrament, as above, are granted: An indulgence of 500 days for each Canonical Hour.

2) The indulgence formerly attached to the recitation of the prayer *Sacrosanctæ*, namely, the remission of all faults committed through human frailty in the recitation of the Divine Office, is now attached to the recitation of the *Antiphona finalis B.M.V.*, with which the Divine Office concludes.

IV. PLAN OF THE SUCCEEDING PAGES

15. We shall now study the individual Hours one by one in the succeeding seven chapters. Our general method of procedure will be to give: (*a*) the structure and content of the various Hours; (*b*) where the various parts are to be found in the breviary; (*c*) how they are to be said; and (*d*) special notes.

Chapter IX is a recapitulation of the preceding seven chapters, a graphic comparative study of the various classes of Offices emphasizing their similarities and differences. It is followed by chapters on the Office of the Dead, on the variations introduced into the Office at special seasons, and on reading the Ordo.

In Part II complete Offices are outlined by way of illustration. These may profitably be consulted after each individual Hour has been studied. References to this section, therefore, will be found in each chapter.

Thus, we shall study the Office first analytically part by part (Chapters II to VIII), then comparatively and as a whole (Chapter IX), and, finally, practically in illustrative Offices (Chapters XIII to XV). The merit of such a method is, we believe, that doubts and difficulties which occur—and each will have his own, different from those of anyone else—will gradually solve themselves as the matter is presented in various ways.

CHAPTER II

MATINS OF THREE NOCTURNS

16. Matins and Lauds together theoretically form the first of the Canonical Hours of the Divine Office. Practically, however, they are two separate Hours, and this justifies us in considering each by itself.

There are two kinds of Matins; namely, Matins of Three Nocturns, and Matins of One Nocturn. We shall consider only the former in the present chapter.

17. When said.—Matins of Three Nocturns is said in the *Officium festivum* and also in the *Officium semi-festivum;* therefore on all feasts of the I and II class.

I. THE CONTENT OF A MATINS OF THREE NOCTURNS

In Matins of Three Nocturns, as in all other Hours, three parts may be distinguished: namely, an introduction, a body, and a conclusion.

18. The Plan of a Matins of Three Nocturns.—

THE INTRODUCTION

The introduction comprises

1) Two introductory verses and responses, namely:

℣. *Dómine, lábia mea apéries.*

℟. *Et os meum annuntiábit laudem tuam.*

11

℣. *Deus, in adiutórium meum inténde.*
℟. *Dómine, ad adiuvándum me festína.*
2) The *Gloria Patri.*
3) *Alleluia.*
4) An invitatory and the psalm 94, *Venite, exsultemus.*
5) A hymn.

THE BODY

The body consists of three nocturns.

The First Nocturn

The first nocturn comprises
1) Three antiphons and psalms, each psalm ending with a *Gloria Patri.*
2) A versicle and response.
3) The *Pater noster.*
4) An absolution.
5) Three lessons, numbered i, ii, iii. Each lesson is introduced by *Iube, Dómine, benedícere* and its own blessing, and followed by *Tu autem, Dómine, miserére nobis, Deo grátias* and its own response and verse.

The Second Nocturn

This is exactly like the first in structure. Its lessons will be numbered iv, v, vi.

The Third Nocturn

This, too, is like the first. Its lessons will be numbered vii, viii, ix. Note, however, that the ninth lesson has no response and verse. Instead, after the *Tu autem,*

Dómine, miserére nobis. Deo grátias, the *Te Deum* is said.

ꜛ

THE CONCLUSION

NOTE. Matins has a conclusion only when Lauds is separated from Matins and said as a separate Hour.

The conclusion, when used, consists of

1) The verse and response
   ℣. *Dómine, exáudi oratiónem meam.*
   ℞. *Et clamor meus ad te véniat.*
2) The oration of the Office of the day preceded by *Orémus.*
3) The verses and responses
   ℣. *Dómine, exáudi oratiónem meam.*
   ℞. *Et clamor meus ad te véniat.*
   ℣. *Benedicámus Dómino.*
   ℞. *Deo grátias.*
   ℣. *Fidélium ánimæ per misericórdiam Dei requiéscant in pace.*
   ℞. *Amen.*

NOTE. It is advisable to commit this plan of Matins to memory. It would, of course, be learnt sooner or later without conscious effort as a result of saying the Office. Yet, if it is memorized now, it will eliminate all necessity of referring to a book to find out what comes next when the saying of the Office is of obligation.

The same is true of the outlines of the other Hours, with the possible exception of Prime and Compline, for these Hours are practically unvarying, though even with regard to these the time thus spent would not be time lost.

II. WHERE THE VARIOUS PARTS ARE FOUND

NOTE. 1) In this and other sections under the same title, no account will be taken of exceptions; only the general rules will be given. All exceptions have been collected in Chapter XI, Seasonal Changes.

2) In what follows, frequent reference will be made to the *Commune Sanctorum*. This means that if the feast is of an Apostle, the *Commune Apostolorum* is to be used; if of a virgin, the *Commune Virginum*; if of the Blessed Virgin, the *Commune B.M.V. per annum*.

3) Many of the parts given in the *Ordinarium* are reprinted for convenience in the *Psalterium* in many modern editions of the breviary. It might be advisable, when first beginning to use the breviary, to take these parts from the *Ordinarium* rather than the *Psalterium* until a certain familiarity with the Office has been acquired.

19. The various parts of a Matins of Three Nocturns are taken from the following sections of the breviary:

1) The introduction from the *Ordinarium*, except the invitatory and its corresponding hymn. These are taken from the *Proprium Sanctorum* if given there; or else from the *Commune Sanctorum*.

2) The three antiphons and psalms for each nocturn and the verse and response after each set of three psalms from the *Proprium Sanctorum* if given there; or else from the *Commune Sanctorum*.

3) The absolution for each set of three lessons and the benedictions, one for each lesson, from the *Ordinarium*.

4) The lessons for each nocturn and the responses

and verses after each lesson from the *Proprium Sanctorum*.

5) The *Te Deum*, which takes the place of the response and verse of the ninth lesson, from the *Ordinarium*.

6) The conclusion, when one is used, from the *Ordinarium*, except for the oration of the Office, which is taken from the *Proprium Sanctorum*.

III. HOW THE VARIOUS PARTS ARE SAID

20. The Introductory Verses and Responses.—At the verse *Dómine, lábia mea apéries*, make the sign of the cross on the lips. At the next verse *Deus, in adiutórium* make the large sign of the cross. As stated before, these ceremonies are not of obligation when saying the Office alone, but the rubrics recommend that they be used.

21. The Invitatory and the Psalm 94, *Venite, exsultemus*.—Before the psalm the invitatory is said twice in full. Then the psalm is begun. After the first and all odd verses of the psalm, the invitatory is repeated in full. After the second and all even verses of the psalm, the last half of the invitatory is said; that is, from the asterisk to the end. After the *Gloria Patri* which concludes the psalm, the last half of the invitatory is said, and then the whole invitatory is repeated once more.

22. The Psalms. *a*) The *Gloria Patri* in full, that is, with *Sicut erat*, must be added as the last verse of all psalms and canticles unless a rubric in the breviary explicitly forbids this addition.

b) An asterik (*) divides each verse of the psalm.
It indicates a pause in the recitation. The pause is of
obligation only when the Office is said in choir or in
common. It is a real help toward achieving a devout
recitation if observed when saying the Office alone.

23. The Antiphons.—The antiphons are always said
in full before and after all psalms and canticles. Whenever an antiphon agrees perfectly in wording with the
first words of the psalm, these words in the psalm are
omitted. A dagger at the end of the antiphon will call
the priest's attention to the identity of wording. Another
dagger in the psalm will indicate the point where the
psalm is to be begun.

24. The Pater Noster.—The *Pater noster* ends with
Amen only when it is to be said *totum secreto*. Therefore, whenever the last verses are printed in the
breviary, the *Amen* is not said.

25. The Lessons.—All titles of lessons must be read.
Therefore, read: *Incipit liber Ecclesiástici*, or *Léctio
Sancti Evangélii secúndum Lucam, Homília Sancti
Gregórii Papœ*, etc.

26. The Response and Verse after each Lesson.—
This response and verse may be printed in any one of
three ways: (*a*) with one asterisk and no *Gloria Patri;*
(*b*) with one asterisk and a *Gloria Patri;* (*c*) with two
asterisks and a *Gloria Patri*. For illustrations confer the
Office *In Festis B.M.V. per Annum*, found toward the
end of the *Commune Sanctorum*. The response and
verse after the first and second lessons of the first
nocturn contain an asterisk but no *Gloria Patri;* after
the third lesson of the first nocturn, an asterisk and a
Gloria Patri; after the third lesson of the second nocturn

(the sixth lesson of the Office), two asterisks and a *Gloria Patri.*

27. The rules, then, for the recitation of the response and verse found after each lesson are the following:

a) If the response and verse are printed with one asterisk and no *Gloria Patri,* read the whole response as printed; then the whole verse; after this, repeat that part of the response which follows the asterisk.

b) If the response and verse are printed with one asterisk and a *Gloria Patri,* read the whole response; then the whole verse; repeat that part of the response which follows the asterisk; say the *Gloria Patri,* but without *Sicut erat;* finally, repeat once more that part of the response which follows the asterisk.

c) If the response and verse are printed with two asterisks and a *Gloria Patri,* read the whole response; then the whole verse; repeat that portion of the response which is included between the two asterisks; say the *Gloria Patri,* but without *Sicut erat;* finally, repeat that portion of the response which follows the second asterisk.

28. Examples.—

1) One asterisk and no *Gloria Patri.*

How printed	*How said*
℟. Sancta et immaculáta virgínitas, quibus te láudibus éfferam néscio: * Quia quem cæli cápere non póterant, tuo grémio contulísti. ℣. Benedícta tu in	Sancta et immaculáta virgínitas, quibus te láudibus éfferam néscio: Quia quem cæli cápere non póterant, tuo grémio contulísti. Benedícta tu in muliéri-

How printed

muliéribus, et benedíctus fructus ventris tui. Quia.

How said

bus, et benedíctus fructus ventris tui. Quia quem cæli cápere non póterant, tuo grémio contulísti.

2) One asterisk and a *Gloria Patri.*

How printed

℞. Beáta es, Virgo María, quæ Dóminum portásti Creatórem mundi: * Genuísti qui te fecit et in ætérnum pérmanes Virgo. ℣. Ave María, grátia plena, Dóminus tecum. Genuísti. Glória Patri. Genuísti.

How said

Beáta es, Virgo María, quæ Dóminum portásti Creatórem mundi: Genuísti qui te fecit, et in ætérnum pérmanes Virgo. Ave María, grátia plena, Dóminus tecum. Genuísti qui te fecit, et in ætérnum pérmanes Virgo. Glória Patri, et Fílio, et Spirítui Sancto. Genuísti qui te fecit, et in ætérnum pérmanes Virgo.

3) Two asterisks and a *Gloria Patri.*

How printed

℞. Ornátam monílibus fíliam Ierúsalem Dóminus concupívit: * Et vidéntes eam fíliæ Sion, beatíssimam prædicavérunt, dicéntes: * Unguéntum ef-

How said

Ornátam monílibus fíliam Ierúsalem Dóminus concupívit: et vidéntes eam fíliæ Sion, beatíssimam prædicavérunt, dicéntes: Unguéntum effúsum no-

How printed

fúsum nomen tuum.
℣. Astitit regína a dextris tuis in vestítu deauráto, circúmdata varietáte.
Et. Glória Patri. Unguéntum.

How said

men tuum. Astitit regína a dextris tuis in vestítu deauráto, circúmdata varietáte. Et vidéntes eam fíliæ Sion, beatíssimam prædicavérunt, dicéntes: Glória Patri, et Fílio, et Spirítui Sancto. Unguéntum effúsum nomen tuum.

IV. SPECIAL NOTES

29. The *Dóminus Vobíscum.*—In the conclusion for Matins as given in the *Ordinarium* you will find the verse and response *Dóminus vobíscum. Et cum spíritu tuo* and not the verse and response we have given, *Dómine, exáudi oratiónem meam. Et clamor meus ad te véniat.* The reason for the discrepancy is the fact that the breviary is printed for the recitation of the Divine Office in choir or in common. Then *Dóminus vobíscum* is used. When saying the Office alone the priest is directed by the rubrics to change the *Dóminus vobíscum* to *Dómine, exáudi oratiónem meam* wherever it occurs in the Office. If this latter immediately precedes the *Dóminus vobíscum* in the text of the Office, then the priest saying the Office alone merely omits the *Dóminus vobíscum.*

For practical illustrations of a Matins of Three Nocturns confer paragraph 137.

CHAPTER III

MATINS OF ONE NOCTURN

30. The Hour of Matins has only one nocturn in the Office of all feasts of the III class, in the Sunday Office, and in the ferial and vigil Offices. This does not mean that the second and third nocturns are merely omitted, but it involves other changes in the Hour as well. We shall now see what these changes are.

I. CONTENT OF A MATINS OF ONE NOCTURN

31. The plan of a Matins of One Nocturn.—

THE INTRODUCTION

The introduction is exactly like the introduction of a Matins of Three Nocturns.

THE BODY

The body of a Matins of One Nocturn comprises

1) Nine antiphons and psalms.
2) A verse and response at their conclusion.
3) The *Pater noster* and an absolution.
4) Three lessons, each preceded by *Iube, Dómine, benedícere* and an appropriate blessing, and fol-

lowed by *Tu autem, Dómine, míserere nobis. Deo grátias.*

5) After the first and second lessons an appropriate response and verse are recited; after the third lesson the *Te Deum* is said except in ferial Offices, when a response and verse are said instead.

THE CONCLUSION

The same rule governs the conclusion of a Matins of One Nocturn that governed that of a Matins of Three Nocturns; in other words, the conclusion is used only when Lauds does not follow immediately upon Matins. The conclusion, when used, is the same as that which terminated a Matins of Three Nocturns.

II. WHERE THE VARIOUS PARTS ARE FOUND

32. For the *Officium dominicale,* or Sunday Office.— The various parts of Matins for this Office are taken from the following sections of the breviary:

1) The introduction from the *Ordinarium,* except for the invitatory and its corresponding hymn. These are taken from the *Psalterium, Dominica ad Matutinum.*

2) The nine antiphons and psalms and the verse and response at their conclusion from the *Psalterium, Dominica ad Matutinum.*

3) The absolution and the blessings for each lesson from the *Ordinarium.*

4) The three lessons with their responses and verses from the *Proprium de Tempore.* Two of these lessons are Scripture Occurring lessons. The third is a homily on the Gospel. For the Sundays after Pentecost this will

be found at the end of the *Proprium de Tempore* and not with the lessons from the Scriptures.

5)   The *Te Deum*, which takes the place of the response and verse after the third lesson, from the *Ordinarium*.

6)   The conclusion, when required, from the *Ordinarium*, except for the oration, which is taken from the *Proprium de Tempore*.

33. For the *Officium ordinarium*, or ordinary Office.—This is the Office of all feasts of the III class. The various parts of Matins for this Office are taken from the following sections of the breviary:

1)   The introduction is from the *Ordinarium* except for the invitatory and its corresponding hymn. These are regularly taken from the *Commune Sanctorum*, very rarely from the *Proprium Sanctorum*.

2)   The nine antiphons and psalms, together with the verse and response at their conclusion, from the *Psalterium* for the current ferial.

3)   The absolution and the blessings before the lessons are taken from the *Ordinarium*.

4)   The first two lessons are from the *Proprium de Tempore* (Scripture Occurring lessons), the third lesson is from the *Proprium Sanctorum*.

5)   The *Te Deum* is from the *Ordinarium*.

6)   The conclusion, if said, is from the *Ordinarium* except for the oration, which is from the *Proprium Sanctorum*.

34. For the *Officium feriale*, or ferial Office.—The various parts of Matins for this Office are taken from the following sections of the breviary:

1) The introduction is from the *Ordinarium* except for the invitatory and its hymn, which are from the *Psalterium*.

2) The nine antiphons and psalms together with the concluding verse and response are all from the *Psalterium*.

3) The absolution and the blessings for the lessons are from the *Ordinarium*.

4) The lessons are from the *Proprium de Tempore*, as are the responses after the lessons.

5) The conclusion when used is from the *Ordinarium* except for the prayer, which is from the *Proprium de Tempore*. It is the oration of the preceding Sunday.

III. HOW THE VARIOUS PARTS ARE SAID

35. The rules and directions given for the recitation of the various parts of a Matins of Three Nocturns apply also to a Matins of One Nocturn.

36. On the Lessons of the Sunday Office.—In the Sunday Office, particularly if you are using an older breviary, note that the first lesson is the first lesson of the Scripture Occurring lessons; the second lesson consists of the second and third Scripture Occurring lessons joined into one. You omit the response and verse found at the end of the second lesson. The response and verse for this combined lesson is the one after the third lesson. This combination of lessons is made for you in the newest breviaries.

37. On the Lessons of the Ordinary Office.—In the *Officium ordinarium* the second lesson is always a combination of the second and third Scripture Occurring lessons joined into one, omitting the response and verse between the two lessons.

38. On the Lessons of the Ferial Office.—In the ferial Office the lessons are from the *Scriptura occurrens* and are read as printed. You do not combine lessons in this Office.

IV. SPECIAL NOTES

39. Scheme I and II.—On Wednesday the ninth psalm of Matins is psalm 50 *Miserere*. When Scheme II is used at Lauds, this psalm will be the first psalm at Lauds. To avoid repetition it is omitted in Matins. To fill up the number of nine psalms for Matins, the preceding psalm 49 is divided into three instead of the usual two parts. The two different arrangements are designated as Scheme I and II. You use Scheme I if you are to say Scheme I at Lauds; otherwise use Scheme II.

40. Special Antiphons and Psalms.—Some few feasts of the III class have special antiphons for the Hour of Matins. When this happens, the psalms are not taken from the *Psalterium* but from the *Commune Sanctorum*. These psalms may be printed with the special antiphons in the *Proprium Sanctorum*. An illustration is the feast of the Apparition of the B.V.Mary on February 11.

41. Special Lessons.—Some few feasts of the III class have special lessons of their own. These are then read instead of the lessons from the *Proprium de Tempore* and in the same way. The *Ordo* will always call attention to the fact when it occurs.

42. Santæ Mariæ in Sabbato.—This Office, found at the end of the *Commune Festorum B.M.V.*, is always said on Saturdays which are ferials of the IV class. There are a special absolution and special blessings for the three lessons of this Office. They are found in the *Commune*. The lessons for the Office are: lesson one from the *Scriptura occurrens* with its response; lesson two is a combination of lessons two and three from the *Scriptura occurrens* with the response from the third; lesson three is proper and found in the *Commune*, a different one for each month of the year.

43. The *Te Deum*.—In the preceding pages we have given merely the general rule which governs the recitation of this hymn; namely, that it is omitted only in ferial Offices. There are, however, exceptions and, since they are numerous, it may not be amiss to give them here. They need, of course, not be learnt, for both the breviary and the Ordo will indicate any deviation from the general rule.

a) The *Te Deum* is not said on the Sundays of Advent or on the Sundays from Septuagesima till Easter exclusive.

b) It is said, even in ferial Offices, from Easter until Pentecost; from Christmas to January 13th; on the vigil of the Ascension.

For practical illustrations of a Matins of One Nocturn confer numbers 147, 155.

CHAPTER IV

LAUDS

44. Lauds is the second half of the first Hour of the Divine Office. In choir it must always be said immediately after Matins except on Christmas day; but when the priest says his Office alone, it may always be separated from Matins.

I. THE CONTENT OF LAUDS

45. The Plan of Lauds.—

THE INTRODUCTION

The introduction consists of

1) An introductory verse and response, namely
   ℣. *Deus, in adiutórium meum inténde.*
   ℟. *Dómine, ad adiuvándum me festína.*
2) The *Glória Patri.*
3) *Allelúia.*

THE BODY

The body comprises

1) Five antiphons and psalms.
2) A *capitulum* followed by the response *Deo grátias.*
3) A hymn followed by a verse and response.

26

4) The antiphon for the *Benedictus*, the *Benedictus* concluded with the *Glória Patri* and a repetition of the antiphon.

5) The *preces* when required.

6) The oration of the Office introduced by
℣. *Dómine, exáudi oratiónem meam.*
℟. *Et clamor meus ad te véniat.*
Orémus.

7) The commemorations if any are to be made.

THE CONCLUSION

Conclude Lauds with the following verses and responses:

℣. *Dómine, exáudi oratiónem meam.*
℟. *Et clamor meus ad te véniat.*
℣. *Benedicámus Dómino.*
℟. *Deo grátias.*
℣. *Fidélium ánimæ per misericórdiam Dei requiéscant in pace.*
℟. *Amen.*

II. WHERE THE VARIOUS PARTS ARE FOUND

NOTE. The introduction and conclusion are always taken from the *Ordinarium*.

46. For the *Officium dominicale.*—

The various parts of Lauds for this Office are taken from the following sections of the breviary:

1) The antiphons for the psalms, the psalms, *capitulum*, hymn, verse and response from the *Psalterium, Dominica ad Laudes.*

2) The antiphon for the *Benedictus* from the *Proprium de Tempore.*

3) The *Benedictus* from the *Ordinarium.*

4)   The introductory verse for the oration from the *Ordinarium*.

5)   The oration of the Office from the *Proprium de Tempore*.

6)   The commemorations, if any are to be made, from the *Proprium Sanctorum*.

47. For the *Officium festivum* and *Officium semi-festivum.—*

The various parts of Lauds for these Offices are taken from the following sections of the breviary:

1)   The antiphons for the psalms from the *Proprium Sanctorum* if given there, or else from the *Commune Sanctorum*.

2)   The psalms from the *Psalterium, Dominica ad Laudes*.

3)   The *capitulum*, hymn, verse, response, and the antiphon for the *Benedictus* from the *Proprium Sanctorum* if given there, or else from the *Commune.*

4)   The *Benedictus* from the *Ordinarium*.

5)   The introductory verse for the oration from the *Ordinarium*.

6)   The oration of the Office and the orations for the commemorations, if any are to be made, from the *Proprium Sanctorum*.

48. For the *Officium ordinarium.—*

The various parts of Lauds for this Office are taken from the following sections of the breviary:

1)   The antiphons and psalms from the *Psalterium*.

2)   The *capitulum*, hymn, verse, response, and the antiphon for the *Benedictus* from the *Commune Sanctorum;* rarely from the *Proprium*.

3)   The *Benedictus* from the *Ordinarium*.

4) The introductory verse for the oration from the *Ordinarium*.

5) The oration of the Office and the orations for the commemorations, if any are to be made, from the *Proprium Sanctorum*.

49. For the *Officium feriale*.—

The various parts of Lauds for this Office are taken from the following sections of the breviary:

1) The psalms and their antiphons, the *capitulum*, hymn, verse, response, and the antiphon for the *Benedictus* from the *Psalterium* for the current ferial.

2) The *Benedictus* from the *Ordinarium*.

3) The introduction to the oration from the *Ordinarium*.

4) The oration in ferial Offices from the *Proprium de Tempore*—it is the prayer of the preceding Sunday; if the ferial Office is of a vigil, from the *Proprium Sanctorum*.

5) A commemoration, if one is to be made, from the *Proprium Sanctorum*.

III. HOW THE VARIOUS PARTS ARE SAID

50. The Introduction.—Make the large sign of the cross at the verse *Deus, in adiutórium*.

51. The Antiphons.—The antiphons are said in full before and after each psalm.

52. The Psalms.—Each psalm concludes with a *Glória Patri*.

53. The Hymn.—The hymns no longer change the last verse to conform to the feast. Always read the hymns as printed.

54. The Benedictus.—Make the large sign of the cross when beginning the *Benedictus*.

55. The Conclusion of the Orations.—As at Mass all orations have the long conclusion. The rules are as follows:

a) If the oration is addressed to the Father, the conclusion is: *Per Dóminum nostrum Iesum Christum Fílium tuum, qui tecum vivit et regnat in unitáte Spíritus Sancti, Deus, per ómnia sæcula sæculórum. Amen.*

b) If the oration is addressed to the Father, but the Son is mentioned in the beginning of the prayer, the conclusion is: *Per eúndem Dóminum nostrum,* etc., as above.

c) If the oration is addressed to the Father, but the Son is mentioned toward the end of the oration, the conclusion is: *Qui tecum vivit et regnat in unitáte Spíritus Sancti, Deus, per ómnia sæcula sæculórum. Amen.*

d) If the oration is addressed to the Son, it concludes with the words: *Qui vivis et regnas cum Deo Patre in unitáte Spíritus Sancti, Deus, per ómnia sæcula sæculórum. Amen.*

e) If the Holy Spirit is mentioned in the oration, use the phrase: *. . . in unitáte eiúsdem Spíritus Sancti* in the conclusion.

Little difficulty will be experienced in the use of these conclusions even though they are not printed in full in the breviary, for the significant words of the conclusion are always given.

56. The Commemorations.—Unlike the commemorations at Mass, which consist merely of an oration, the commemorations in the Divine Office have three parts; namely, an antiphon, a verse with its response, and a prayer always preceded by *Orémus*. The antiphon for the commemorations at Lauds is the antiphon of the *Benedictus*. However, it is not the antiphon which has already been used with the *Benedictus*, but the antiphon which would have been used had the Office of the feast commemorated been said. This antiphon, therefore, must be taken from the *Commune Sanctorum*. However, most breviaries reprint it in the *Proprium Sanctorum* together with the oration of the Office. The verse and response that must be said are the verse and response found immediately before the antiphon used. If the antiphon has been reprinted in the *Proprium Sanctorum*, the verse and response will also be found there immediately after the antiphon. Only the oration of the Office and the oration of the last commemoration have a conclusion.

There is one significant exception to the above rule for commemorations. In any Office of St. Peter, St. Paul is always commemorated by adding the oration of St. Paul to that of St. Peter under one conclusion and without either antiphon or verse and response. The same applies to any Office of St. Paul. In it St. Peter is commemorated in the same way. The two prayers joined together under one conclusion count only as one prayer.

57. As a practical illustration of the procedure to be followed when commemorations occur, let us consider an Office in which two commemorations are to be made. Let us suppose that the Office of the feast is the Office of a Confessor, and that a Martyr and a Virgin are to be commemorated. After the recitation of the *Benedictus* and the repetition of the antiphon of the *Bene• dictus*, proceed as follows:

1) Recite the following verse and response:
   ℣. *Dómine, exáudi oratiónem meam.*
   ℟. *Et clamor meus ad te véniat.*
   ℣. *Orémus.*

2) Say the oration of the Office of the day. This oration is taken from the *Proprium Sanctorum* and has a conclusion.

3) For the first commemoration of the Martyr say:
   a) The antiphon of the *Benedictus* taken from the *Commune Unius Martyris*, which begins with the words *Qui odit.*
   b) The verse and response which immediately precede this antiphon in the same *Commune: Iustus ut palma. Sicut cedrus.*
   c) *Orémus.*
   d) The oration in honor of the Martyr. It will have no conclusion since another commemoration is to follow. The oration is found in the *Proprium Sanctorum.*

4) For the second commemoration of the Virgin say:
   a) The antiphon of the *Benedictus* taken from the *Commune Virginum: Date ei.*
   b) The verse and response which precede it: *Diffúsa est. Proptérea.*
   c) *Orémus.*
   d) The oration in honor of the Virgin. It will have a conclusion, since it is the last commemora-

tion. The oration is found in the *Proprium Sanctorum*.

58. ' A difficulty may occur if the saint to be commemorated has the same *Commune* as the one whose Office is being said, because one may not use the same antiphon twice in any hour. A complicated set of rules is given for such cases. (Cf. Special Notes, paragraph 62.) In practice, however, there is no difficulty, for the Ordo will always indicate which antiphon, verse, and response is to be used in such cases if the breviary has not already taken care of the situation by printing what is needed in full.

59. A similar difficulty may occur with regard to the prayer of the commemoration. Should this prayer be identical with the oration of the Office or with an oration of a commemoration already made, another prayer must be chosen from among those given in the *Commune*.

IV. SPECIAL NOTES

60. Scheme I and II of Lauds.—The breviary prints two sets of psalms for Lauds. The second set is used on days which have a penitential character. Thus, scheme II is used on the Sundays from Septuagesima to the second Passion Sunday inclusive. It is also used in the ferial Offices of Advent and in ferial Offices from Septuagesima to the second Passion Sunday; in the ferial Office of the Ember Days of September; in the ferial Office of vigils of the II and III class outside of Paschaltide. The Ordo will always indicate which scheme is to be used.

61. The Preces.—*Preces* are recited only in some ferial Offices. These are the ferial Offices of the Ember Days, except those of Pentecost; the Wednesdays and Fridays of Advent and Lent.

62. Commemorations from the same Commune.

a) If only one commemoration is to be made from the same *Commune* from which the Office of the day is taken, use the antiphon, verse and response found in I Vespers.

b) If two commemorations are to be made from the same *Commune* but not from the *Commune* from which the Office of the day is taken, then the antiphon, verse and response from Lauds are used for the first commemoration; those from I Vespers are used for the second.

c) If two commemorations are to be made from the same *Commune* from which the Office for the day is taken, the first commemoration takes its antiphon, verse and response from I Vespers, the second commemoration from II Vespers. But note that if the antiphons for I and II Vespers are the same, use for the antiphon the first antiphon of the psalms for the third nocturn.

63. Commemorating a Vigil.—When commemorating a vigil, the antiphon, verse and response are taken from the Psalterium for the current ferial.

For practical illustrations of Lauds confer paragraphs 138, 148, 156.

CHAPTER V

PRIME

64. Prime is the first of the four Small Hours. Though it differs considerably from the other Small Hours, nevertheless it is not a difficult Hour to recite, as most of its parts are invariable and recited as printed in the breviary.

I. THE CONTENT OF PRIME

65. The Plan of Prime.—

THE INTRODUCTION

The introduction consists of

1) The introductory verse and response
℣. *Deus, in adiutórium meum inténde.*
℟. *Dómine, ad adiuvándum me festína.*
2) The *Glória Patri.*
3) *Allelúia.*
4) An invariable hymn *Iam lucis orto.*

THE BODY

The body comprises

1) An antiphon said in full.
2) Three psalms.

3) A repetition of the antiphon.
4) A *capitulum* concluded with *Deo grátias.*
5) A *responsorium breve* followed by a verse and ‧ response.
6) The invariable oration of Prime followed by a con-ᛋ clusion as though the Hour ended there.
7) A verse and response followed by a sequence of prayers and ending with
8) The *lectio brevis,* preceded by *Iube, Dómine, bene-dícere* and an invariable benediction, and followed by *Tu autem, Dómine, miserére nobis. Deo grátias.*

THE CONCLUSION

Prime is concluded with

1) the verses and responses
   ℣. *Adiutórium nostrum in nómine Dómini.*
   ℞. *Qui fecit cœlum et terram.*
   ℣. *Benedícite.*
   ℞. *Deus.*
2) The benediction: *Dóminus nos benedícat.*

II. WHERE THE VARIOUS PARTS ARE FOUND

NOTE. The introduction and conclusion are always taken from the *Ordinarium.*

66. For the *Officium dominicale.*—

The various parts of Prime for this Office are taken from the following sections of the breviary:

1) The antiphon and psalms from the *Psalterium, Dominica ad Primam.*

2) All the rest from the *Ordinarium.*

67. For the *Officium festivum.*—

The various parts of Prime for this Office are taken from the following sections of the breviary:

1) The antiphon from the *Proprium Sanctorum.* It is the first one of those used at Lauds.

2) The three psalms from the *Psalterium, Dominica ad Primam.* Note, however, that the psalms ordinarily said in Sunday's Prime are psalms 117, and 118^1, 118^2. In the *Officium festivum* psalm 117 is omitted and psalm 53, which is printed immediately after psalm 117, is said instead. This is what is meant by the rubric in festal Offices at Prime: *Psalmi de Dominica, ad Primam tamen ut in festis.*

3) All the rest, including the *lectio brevis,* from the *Ordinarium.*

68. For the *Officium semifestivum, ordinarium, feriale.*—

The various parts of Prime for these Offices are taken from the following sections of the breviary:

1) The antiphon and psalms from the *Psalterium* for the current ferial.

2) All the rest from the *Ordinarium.*

III. HOW THE VARIOUS PARTS ARE SAID

69. Make the sign of the cross at the introductory verse *Deus, in adiutórium.*

70. The antiphon is said in full before the first psalm. Each psalm ends with the *Glória Patri.* After the last psalm the antiphon is repeated.

71. The Responsorium Breve.—We shall find *responsoria brevia* in all the Small Hours; that is, in

Prime, Terce, Sext, None, and also in Compline. Each
responsorium breve consists of a brief response punctu-
ated by an asterisk. After this the first word or words
of the response are reprinted. Then comes a verse. This
is followed by the first word or two of that part of the
response following the asterisk. Next are the words
Glória Patri. Then again the first word or two of the
response. Finally there is another verse and response.
To recite the *responsorium breve* read the response up
to the verse twice. Next say the verse. Repeat the
second half of the response; that is, from the asterisk
to the verse. Say the *Glória Patri* but without the *Sicut
erat*. Repeat the whole response up to the verse. Then
say the last verse and response.

All this sounds very complicated and probably is.
An illustration should make the matter clear. We illus-
trate with the *responsorium breve* of Prime.

How printed

℟. br. Christe, Fili Dei
vivi. * Miserére nobis.
Christe. ℣. Qui sedes ad
déxteram Patris. Miserére
nobis. Glória Patri. Christe.

℣. Exsúrge, Christe, ádi-
uva nos. ℟. Et líbera nos
propter nomen tuum.

How said

Christe, Fili Dei vivi. Mi-
serére nobis. Christe, Fili
Dei vivi. Miserére nobis.
Qui sedes ad déxteram
Patris. Miserére nobis.
Glória Patri et Fílio et
Spirítui Sancto. Christe,
Fili Dei vivi. Miserére
nobis.

Exsúrge, Christe, ádiuva
nos. Et líbera nos propter
nomen tuum.

72. The Conclusion.—At the words *Adiutórium nostrum* make the large sign of the cross. Again at the benediction *Dóminus nos benedícat.*

IV. SPECIAL NOTES

73. A careful analysis of the Hour of Prime will reveal the fact that it really consists of two parts. When the monks of old recited Prime, they said the first part of this Hour in choir. This part ends with the oration of Prime followed by the usual conclusion of a Small Hour. The second part of Prime was recited in the chapter room. It began with the reading of the Martyrology. The work for the day was then assigned to the monks. Hence the many requests for help and blessing on their work which fills the remaining part of this Hour. The rubric in this part of Prime now reads *Deinde in choro legitur Martyrologium, quod convenientur fit etiam extra chorum.* Certainly it is not even an imperfection to omit the Martyrology. It is a reason, though, why the Martyrology is still read in the refectories of Religious Communities at dinner.

74. Sunday Prime When Scheme II Is Used at Lauds.—The first psalm of the Hour of Prime on Sunday is psalm 117. This appears as one of the psalms of Lauds in Scheme II for Sunday. To avoid repetition, psalm 53 is said in Prime instead of psalm 117 when Scheme II is used at Lauds. The Ordo will remind the priest when this has to be done.

75. The *Quicumque.*—On the Feast of the Most Holy Trinity the Creed attributed to St. Athanasius and which begins with the word *Quicumque* is added to the

Hour of Prime after the third psalm and before the antiphon is repeated. The *Glória Patri* concludes the *Quicumque* just as though it were a psalm. Then the antiphon is recited.

76. The *Responsorium Breve.*—The verse in the *responsorium breve* of Prime, namely, *Qui sedes ad déxteram Patris,* is changed with the season and for certain feasts. Thus, on feasts of the Blessed Virgin, the verse is changed to *Qui natus es de María Vírgine*. The verse to be used is found in the *Proprium Sanctorum* for all feasts which are not of the Blessed Virgin. Both breviary and Ordo will call attention to any change of the verse which has to be made.

For practical illustrations of the Hour of Prime confer paragraphs 139, 149, 157.

CHAPTER VI

TERCE, SEXT, NONE

77. Terce, Sext, and None are the third, fourth, and fifth of the Canonical Hours of the Divine Office respectively. These Hours are identical in structure and may therefore be treated together.

I. THE CONTENT OF TERCE, SEXT, AND NONE

78. The Plan of These Hours.—

THE INTRODUCTION

The introduction consists of

1) The introductory verse and response
℣. *Deus, in adiutórium meum inténde.*
℟. *Dómine, ad adiuvándum me festína.*
2) The *Glória Patri.*
3) *Allelúia.*
4) An invariable hymn.

THE BODY

The body is composed of

1) An antiphon, followed by three psalms, each concluded with *Glória Patri,* after which the antiphon is repeated.

2) A *capitulum* followed by *Deo grátias*.

3) A *responsorium breve* with its verse and response.

4) The oration of the Office, preceded by *Dómine, exáudi oratiónem meam. Et clamor meus ad te véniat. Orémus.*

THE CONCLUSION

The conclusion comprises

1) The verses and responses

℣. *Dómine, exáudi oratiónem meam.*

℟. *Et clamor meus ad te véniat.*

℣. *Benedicámus Dómino.*

℟. *Deo grátias.*

℣. *Fidélium ánimæ per misericórdiam Dei requiéscant in pace.*

℟. *Amen.*

II. WHERE THE VARIOUS PARTS ARE FOUND

Note. The introduction and conclusion are always taken from the *Ordinarium*.

79. For the *Officium dominicale.—*

The various parts of the Small Hours for this Office are taken from the following sections of the breviary:

1) The antiphon and the three psalms from the *Psalterium*.

2) The *capitulum* and *responsorium breve* from the *Ordinarium*, but usually reprinted in the *Psalterium*.

3) The oration from the *Proprium de Tempore*.

80. For the *Officium festivum.—*

The various parts of the Small Hours for this Office are taken from the following sections of the breviary:

1) The antiphon for the psalms from the *Proprium Sanctorum* if given there; otherwise from the *Commune*. One of the antiphons for Lauds is used. The second one is taken for Terce, the third for Sext, and the fifth for None.

2) The psalms from the *Psalterium*. The psalms given for the Small Hours of Sunday are to be used.

3) The *capitulum, responsorium breve,* and the oration of the Office from the *Proprium Sanctorum* if given there; otherwise from the *Commune*.

81. For the *Officium semifestivum.*—

The various parts of the Small Hours for this Office are taken from the following sections of the breviary:

1) The antiphon and the three psalms from the *Psalterium* for the current ferial.

2) The *capitulum* and *responsorium breve* from the *Proprium Sanctorum;* if not given there, from the *Commune*.

3) The oration of the feast from the *Proprium Sanctorum*.

82. For the *Officium ordinarium.*—

The various parts of the Small Hours for this Office are taken from the following sections of the breviary:

1) The antiphon and the three psalms from the *Psalterium* for the current ferial.

2) The *capitulum* and *responsorium breve* from the *Commune*.

3) The oration of the feast from the *Proprium Sanctorum*.

83. For the *Officium feriale.*—

The various parts of the Small Hours for this Office are taken from the following sections of the breviary:

1) The antiphon and the three psalms from the *Psalterium* for the current ferial.

2) The *capitulum* and *responsorium breve* from the *Ordinarium*, but usually reprinted in the *Psalterium*.

3) The oration of the Office, if the Office is of a ferial, from the *Proprium de Tempore*—it is the prayer of the preceding Sunday; if the Office is of a vigil, from the *Proprium*.

III. HOW THE VARIOUS PARTS ARE SAID

84. The large sign of the cross is made in the introduction at the verse *Deus, in adiutórium*. The antiphon is said only before the first psalm and after the third psalm. Each psalm ends with the *Glória Patri*. The *responsoria brevia* are said just like the *responsorium breve* in Prime. Confer paragraph 71.

For practical illustrations of the hour of
Terce, confer paragraphs 140, 150, 158;
Sext, confer paragraphs, 141, 151, 159;
None, confer paragraphs 142, 152, 160.

CHAPTER VII

VESPERS

85. Vespers is the sixth of the Canonical Hours of the Divine Office. It is worth noting that Vespers is practically identical in structure with the Hour of Lauds.

I. THE CONTENT OF THE HOUR OF VESPERS

86. The Plan of Vespers.—

THE INTRODUCTION

The introduction consists of

1) The introductory verse and response.
   ℣. *Deus, in adiutórium meum inténde.*
   ℟. *Dómine, ad adiuvándum me festína.*
2) The *Glória Patri.*
3) *Allelúia.*

THE BODY

The body of Vespers is composed of

1) Five psalms, each preceded by an antiphon and followed by the *Glória Patri* and a repetition of the antiphon.
2) A *capitulum* followed by *Deo grátias.*

3) A hymn followed by a verse and response.
4) The canticle *Magnificat* preceded by its antiphon and followed by the *Glória Patri* and a repetition of the antiphon.
5) The *preces* when required.
6) The oration of the Office preceded by *Dómine, exáudi oratiónem meam. Et clamor meus ad te véniat. Orémus.*
7) The commemorations if any are to be made.

THE CONCLUSION

The conclusion comprises the verses and responses

℣. *Dómine, exáudi oratiónem meam.*
℞. *Et clamor meus ad te véniat.*
℣. *Benedicámus Dómino.*
℞. *Deo grátias.*
℣. *Fidélium ánimæ per misericórdiam Dei requiéscant in pace.*
℞. *Amen.*

II. WHERE THE VARIOUS PARTS ARE FOUND

NOTE. The introduction and conclusion are always taken from the *Ordinarium.*

87. For the *Officium dominicale.*—

The various parts of Vespers for this Office are taken from the following sections of the breviary:

1) The antiphons, psalms, *capitulum*, hymn, verse, and response from the *Psalterium, Dominica ad Vesperas.*

2) The antiphon for the *Magnificat* from the *Proprium de Tempore.*

3) The *Magnificat* from the *Ordinarium*.

4) The oration of the Office from the *Proprium de Tempore*.

5)' The commemorations, if any are to be made, from the *Proprium Sanctorum*.

88. For the *Officium festivum* and *semifestivum.*— The various parts of Vespers for these Offices are taken from the following sections of the breviary:

1) The antiphons, the psalms, *capitulum*, hymn, verse, response, and the antiphon for the *Magnificat* from the *Proprium Sanctorum;* if not given there, from the *Commune*.

2) The *Magnificat* from the *Ordinarium*.

3) The oration of the Office and the commemorations, if any are to be made, from the *Proprium Sanctorum*.

89. For the *Officium ordinarium.*— The various parts of Vespers for this Office are taken from the following sections of the breviary:

1) The antiphons and psalms from the *Psalterium* for the current ferial.

2) The *capitulum*, hymn, verse, response, and the antiphon for the *Magnificat* from the *Commune Sanctorum*.

3) The *Magnificat* from the *Ordinarium*.

4) The oration of the Office and the commemorations if any are to be made, from the *Proprium Sanctorum*.

90. For the *Officium feriale.*— The various parts of Vespers for this Office are taken from the following sections of the breviary:

1) The antiphons, psalms, *capitulum*, hymn, verse,

response, and the antiphon for the *Magnificat* from the *Psalterium* for the current ferial.

2) The *Magnificat*, and *preces* when required, from the *Ordinarium*.

3) The oration of the Office from the *Proprium de Tempore*. It is the prayer of the preceding Sunday.

III. HOW THE VARIOUS PARTS ARE SAID

91. The Introduction.—Make the large sign of the cross at the verse *Deus, in adiutórium*.

92. The antiphons are said in full before and after each psalm, which concludes with the *Glória Patri*.

93. The *Magnificat*.—Make the large sign of the cross when beginning the *Magnificat*.

94. The Commemorations.—The commemorations are made as at Lauds. (Cf. nn. 56-59.) Therefore each prayer is preceded by an antiphon, verse, response, and *Orémus*. The antiphon is the antiphon for the *Magnificat* that would have been used had the Office of the saint to be commemorated been recited. It will be found in the *Commune Sanctorum*, though most breviaries reprint it in the *Proprium Sanctorum*. The verse and response are found immediately before the antiphon in the *Commune*; if reprinted in the *Proprium*, immediately after it.

IV. SPECIAL NOTES

95. First and Second Vespers.—A glance at any of the complete Offices in the *Commune Sanctorum* reveals the fact that two sets of variable parts are given for the Hour of Vespers, one printed immediately before Matins and called First Vespers, the other in the usual place after the Small Hours and called Second Vespers. This does not mean that Vespers is to be said twice on any one day, but that certain of the more important feasts may encroach on the Office of the feast that precedes them and displace its Second Vespers. For instance, suppose that on Monday a feast of the III class is celebrated, while on Tuesday there is a feast of the I class. Then Monday's feast will have no Second Vespers. Instead the First Vespers of Tuesday's feast will be recited on Monday. Only the Sunday Office, the Office of feasts of the I class, and the Office of feasts of the II class if they be feasts of Our Lord and fall on Sunday have First Vespers. The Ordo will always indicate which Vespers is to be said by phrases such as: *Vesperæ festi; Vesperæ sequentis; Vesperæ sequentis, commemoratio præcedentis*, etc.

96. First Vespers of Sunday.—The *Officium dominicale* has First Vespers. It is recited on Saturday, and the antiphons and psalms are taken not from Sunday but from Saturday. The Hour of Compline following First Vespers of the Sunday Office is also taken from Saturday and not from Sunday.

97. Commemorations.—The only commemorations made in Vespers are the privileged commemorations. They are (*a*) of a Sunday; (*b*) of a liturgical day of the I class; (*c*) of days within the octave of Christmas; (*d*) of the Ember Days of September; (*e*) of the ferials of Lent and Advent. All other commemorations

are called ordinary commemorations and are never
made in Vespers.

For practical illustrations of the Hour of Vespers.
confer paragraphs 135, 143, 145, 153, 161.

CHAPTER VIII

COMPLINE

98. Compline is the seventh and last of the Canonical Hours of the Divine Office. In structure it is the most irregular of all the Hours. Its parts, however, are practically invariable and found, for the most part, in the *Ordinarium*. It is therefore one of the easiest Hours to learn.

I. THE CONTENT OF THE HOUR OF COMPLINE

99. The Plan of Compline.—

THE INTRODUCTION

The introduction consists of

1) The verse and benediction
℣. *Iube, Dómine, benedícere.*
Bened. *Noctem quiétam ... Amen.*
2) An invariable *lectio brevis*, followed by *Tu autem, Dómine, miserére nobis. Deo grátias.*
3) The verse and response
℣. *Adiutórium nostrum in nómine Dómini.*
℞. *Qui fecit cœlum et terram.*
4) The *Pater noster* ending with *Amen.*

5) The *Confíteor* followed by the *Misereátur* and *Indulgéntiam.*
6) The verses and responses
　　℣. *Convérte nos, Deus, salutáris noster.*
　　℟. *Et avérte iram tuam a nobis.*
　　℣. *Deus, in adiutórium meum inténde.*
　　℟. *Dómine, ad adiuvándum me festína.*
7) The *Glória Patri.*
8) *Allelúia.*

THE BODY

The body of the Hour of Compline is composed of

1) An antiphon recited before the first psalm and after the third psalm.
2) Three psalms, each concluded with the *Glória Patri.*
3) An invariable hymn.
4) A *capitulum* followed by *Deo grátias.*
5) A *responsorium breve* with its verse and response.
6) The Canticle of Simeon *Nunc dimíttis* preceded by an antiphon and followed by *Glória Patri* with a repetition of the antiphon.
7) An invariable oration preceded by *Dómine, exáudi oratiónem meam. Et clamor meus ad te véniat. Orémus.*

THE CONCLUSION

The conclusion comprises

1) The verses and responses
　　℣. *Dómine, exáudi oratiónem meam.*
　　℟. *Et clamor meus ad te véniat.*
　　℣. *Benedicámus Dómino.*
　　℟. *Deo grátias.*

2) The benediction: *Benedícat et custódiat nos omnípotens et miséricors Dóminus, Pater, et Fílius, et Spíritus Sanctus. Amen.*

3) 'The *Antiphona finalis* of the Blessed Virgin Mary.

4) The verse and response

℣. *Divínum auxílium máneat semper nobíscum.*
℟. *Amen.*

II. WHERE THE VARIOUS PARTS ARE FOUND

100. Everything is taken from the *Ordinarium* (usually reprinted in the *Psalterium*) with one exception; namely, the three psalms and their antiphon. With regard to these observe the following rule: On Sundays, on feasts of the I and II class use the antiphon and psalms from the *Psalterium, Dominica ad Completorium;* in all other Offices take the antiphon and psalms from the *Psalterium* for the current ferial.

III. HOW THE VARIOUS PARTS ARE SAID

101. The Introduction.—Make the large sign of the cross three times during the introduction, namely, at the verse *Adiutórium nostrum;* again at the *Indulgéntiam* after the *Confiteor;* and finally at the verse *Deus, in adiutórium.*

Make a sign of the cross on the breast at the words *Convérte nos.*

102. *The Confiteor.*—When saying the Office alone, omit the words *et vobis, fratres* and *et vos, fratres* in the *Confiteor.*

103. The *Misereatur* and *Indulgentiam.*—When saying the Office alone these prayers are said in the first person plural. Hence *Misereátur nostri* and *remissiónem, peccatórum nostrórum.*

104. The Canticle of Simeon.—Make the large sign of the cross at the beginning of the Canticle of Simeon *Nunc dimittis.*

105. The Conclusion.—Make the large sign of the cross at the benediction *Benedícat et custódiat,* and again at the verse *Divínum auxílium.*

IV. SPECIAL NOTES

106. Compline As Night Prayer.—A rubric strongly recommends that Compline be recited just before retiring as the final prayer of the day, and this also by those who say the Office alone. When this is done, the *Pater noster* immediately preceding the *Confiteor* is omitted. In its place an examination of conscience is made for a reasonable length of time. Then the *Confiteor* is recited and the rest of the Hour said in the usual manner.

For illustrations of the Hour of Compline confer paragraphs 136, 146, 162.

CHAPTER IX

RECAPITULATION

107. We have thus far studied in detail each individual Hour of the Divine Office as said on Sundays, on feasts of the I, II, III classes, and in the ferial Office. It may not be amiss to recapitulate briefly all that we have seen and to study the five kinds of Offices comparatively, pointing out their differences and similarities.

I. SOME GENERALIZATIONS

108. Some Useful General Principles

1) Antiphons and Psalms.—Whenever the psalms are to be taken from the current ferial, the antiphons also are taken from the ferial. If a festal Office of any rank has proper antiphons for Matins, and/or Lauds, and/or Vespers, never use the psalms from the current ferial; but, if none are given with the antiphons, use the psalms from the *Commune* for Matins and Vespers, and from Sunday Lauds for Lauds.

2) The *Glória Patri* is always said in full; that is, with *Sicut erat*, except in two instances; namely, in the responses after the lessons of Matins and in the *responsoria brevia* found in Prime, Terce, Sext, None, and Compline, when the *Sicut erat* is omitted.

3) The response *Tu autem, Dómine, miserére nobis. Deo grátias* concludes all lessons of the Hour of Matins; also all *lectiones breves.* There is one in Prime and one in Compline.

4) The response *Deo grátias* concludes all *capitula.* They are found in all Hours except Matins.

5) The conclusion for Matins must be taken from the *Ordinarium,* with the oration from the *Proprium.* If you anticipate Matins, you will need this conclusion, since you may not anticipate Lauds. It would be well to memorize the conclusion.

II. THE DIVINE OFFICE IN OUTLINE

SIGNS AND ABBREVIATIONS

+ = Large sign of cross
+ = Small sign of cross
I: *Officium festivum*
II: *Officium semifestivum*
III: *Officium ordinarium*
C S: *Commune Sanctorum*
DOM: *Officium dominicale*
FER: *Officium feriale*
Gl. P.: *Gloria Patri*

L 1: Lauds, antiphon 1
L 2, 3, 5: Lauds, 2nd 3rd, 5th
   antiphons
Ord: *Ordinarium*
P d T: *Proprium de Tempore*
P S: *Proprium Sanctorum*
Ps D: *Psalterium Dominicae*
Ps F: *Psalterium ferias*

109. MATINS

	I	II	III	DOM	FER
Domine, labia + mea	Ord	Ord	Ord	Ord	Ord
+ Deus, in adjutorium	"	"	"	"	"
Gloria Patri. Alleluia	"	"	"	"	"
Invitatory (twice)	P S	P S	C S	Ps D	Ps F
Venite	Ord	Ord	Ord	Ord	Ord
Hymn	P S	P S	C S	Ps D	Ps F
THE FIRST NOCTURN					
Ant., Psalm, Gl. P., Ant. }3	P S	P S	Ps F	Ps D	Ps F
Verse and Response	P S	P S			

	I	II	III	DOM	FER
Pater noster (no Amen)	Ord	Ord			
Absolution	"	"			
Iube, Domine. Blessing ⎫	"	"			
Lesson. Tu autem. ⎬3	P S	P S			
Response and Verse ⎭	"	"			

THE SECOND NOCTURN

	I	II	III	DOM	FER
Ant., Psalm, Gl. P., Ant. ⎱3	P S	P S	Ps F	Ps D	Ps F
Verse and Response	"	"			
Pater noster (no Amen)	Ord	Ord			
Absolution	"	"			
Iube, Domine. Blessing ⎫	"	"			
Lesson. Tu autem. ⎬3	P S	P S			
Response and Verse ⎭	"	"			

THE THIRD NOCTURN

	I	II	III	DOM	FER
Ant., Psalm, Gl. P., Ant. ⎱3	"	"	Ps F	Ps D	Ps F
Verse and Response	"	"	"	"	"
Pater noster. Absolution	Ord	Ord	Ord	Ord	Ord
Iube, Domine. Blessing ⎫	"	"	"	"	"
Lesson. Tu autem ⎬2	P S	P S	P d T	P d T	P d T
Response and Verse ⎭	"	"	"	"	"
Iube, Domine. Blessing	Ord	Ord	Ord	Ord	Ord
Lesson. Tu autem	P S	P S	P S	P d T	P d T
Te Deum or Response	Te D	Te D	Te D	Te D	Resp

If You Stop

	I	II	III	DOM	FER
Domine, exaudi	Ord	Ord	Ord	Ord	Ord
Oremus. Oration	P S	P S	P S	P d T	Of Sun.
Domine, exaudi.	Ord	Ord	Ord	Ord	Ord
Benedicamus Domino.	"	"	"	"	"
Fidelium animæ.	"	"	"	"	"

110. LAUDS

	I	II	III	DOM	FER
+ Deus in adiutorium.	Ord	Ord	Ord	Ord	Ord
Gloria Patri. Alleluia.	"	"	"	"	"
Antiphon ⎫	P S	P S	Ps F	Ps D	Ps F
Psalm. Gl. P. ⎬5	Ps D	Ps D	"	"	"
Antiphon ⎭	P S	P S	"	"	"
Capit., hymn, Verse, Response	"	"	C S	"	"
Ant. for Benedictus	"	"	"	P d T	"
+ Benedictus. Gl. P.	Ord	Ord	Ord	Ord	Ord
Ant. for Benedictus	P S	P S	C S	P d T	Ps F

	I	II	III	DOM	FER
Preces if required					Ord
Domine, exaudi.	Ord	Ord	Ord	Ord	"
Oremus. Oration.	P S	P S	P S	P d T	Of Sun.
Commemorations thus:					
Ant. Verse, Oremus, Oration		P S	P S	P S	P S
Domine, exaudi. Benedicamus					
D.	Ord	Ord	Ord	Ord	Ord
Fidelium animæ	"	"	"	"	"

111. PRIME

	I	II	III	DOM	FER
+ Deus, in adiutorium	Ord	Ord	Ord	Ord	Ord
Gl. P. Alleluia. Hymn	"	"	"	"	"
Antiphon	L 1	Ps F	Ps F	Ps D	Ps F
3 Psalms. Gl. P. after each	Ps D	"	"	"	"
Antiphon	L 1	"	"	"	"
Capitulum. Deo gratias	Ord	Ord	Ord	Ord	Ord
Responsorium breve	"	"	"	"	"
Domine, exaudi. Prayers of					
Prime		"	"		
Lectio brevis. Tu autem.		"	"		
+ Adiutorium nostrum.		"	"		
Benedicite. Deus.		"	"		
+ Dominus nos benedicat.		"	"		

112. TERCE, SEXT, NONE.

	I	II	III	DOM	FER
+ Deus, in adiutorium	Ord	Ord	Ord	Ord	Ord
Gloria Patri. Alleluia. Hymn	"	"	"	"	"
Antiphon	L 2, 3,	Ps F	Ps F	Ps D	Ps F
	5				
Psalms, Gloria Patri. ⊹ 3	Ps D		"		"
Antiphon	L 2, 3,		"		"
	5				
Capitulum. Deo gratias.	P S	P S	C S	Ord	Ord
Responsorium breve.	"	"	"	"	"
Domine, exaudi.	Ord	Ord	P S	Ord	Ord
Oremus. Oration	P S	P S	Ord	P d T	Of Sun.
Domine, exaudi.	Ord	Ord	"	Ord	Ord
Benedicamus Domino.	"	"	"	"	"
Fidelium animæ.	"	"	"	"	"

113. VESPERS

Vespers is just like Lauds except that the *Benedictus* is to be changed to the *Magnificat;* that the psalms for the *Officium festivum* and the *Officium semifestivum* are to be taken from the feast and not from Sunday Lauds.

114. COMPLINE

	I	II	III	DOM	FER
Iube, Domine. Noctem quietam.	Ord	Ord	Ord	Ord	Ord
Fratres: Sobrii.	"	"	"	"	"
+ Adiutorium nostrum.	"	"	"	"	"
Pater noster. Amen.	"	"	"	"	"
Confiteor. Misereatur.	"	"	"	"	"
+Indulgentiam.	"	"	"	"	"
Converte nos + (on the breast)	"	"	"	"	"
+ Deus, in adiutorium.	"	"	"	"	"
Gloria Patri. Alleluia.	"	"	"	"	"
Antiphon (in full)	Ps D	Ps D	Ps F	Ps D	Ps F
Psalms. Gl. P. } 3	"	"	"	"	"
Antiphon	"	"	"	"	"
Hymn. Capitulum. Deo gratias	Ord	Ord	Ord	Ord	Ord
Responsorium breve.	"	"	"	"	"
Ant. Salva nos. (in full)	"	"	"	"	"
+ Nunc Dimittis.	"	"	"	"	"
Ant. Salva nos.	"	"	"	"	"
Domine, exaudi.	"	"	"	"	"
Oremus. Visita.	"	"	"	"	"
Domine, exaudi.	"	"	"	"	"
Benedicamus Domino.	"	"	"	"	"
+ Benedicat et custodiat.	"	"	"	"	"
Antiphona finalis B.M.V.	"	"	"	"	"
+ Divinum auxilium.	"	"	"	"	"

CHAPTER X

THE OFFICE OF THE DEAD

115. The Office of the Dead is found at the end of the *Commune Sanctorum*. It has but three Hours, Vespers, Matins, and Lauds, and is never of obligation outside of choir except on November 2, the Commemoration of All the Faithful Departed. On that day it is the Office for the day and is said as an *Officium festivum*. The missing Hours of the Office are supplied for that day in the *Proprium Sanctorum*. On the day of burial the Hour of Matins (the first nocturn only) and the Hour of Lauds are frequently said before the funeral Mass, particularly of priests and Religious. The Office of the Dead may be added, *devotionis causa*, to the obligatory Office. "It is a holy and wholesome thought to pray for the dead that they may be loosed from sins." The usual mode of procedure is to say Vespers after Vespers, and Matins and Lauds after Matins and Lauds. If the whole of Matins for the dead is not recited, then the first nocturn is used on Sundays, Mondays, and Thursdays; the second nocturn on Tuesdays and Fridays; the third nocturn on Wednesdays and Saturdays.

116. In the Office of the Dead the psalms are not concluded with the *Gloria Patri* but with the verse and response *Requiem ætérnam dona eis, Dómine. Et lux perpétua lúceat eis.* The plural number is to be used even though the Office is recited for a particular individual.

117. VESPERS

1) Vespers lacks the usual introduction. It begins with the antiphons and psalms.

2) There is no *capitulum* or hymn after the psalms, just a verse and response.

3) The *Magnificat* is concluded like the psalms with *Réquiem ætérnam.*

4) A special conclusion is used to end the Hour. It consists of:

a) The *Pater noster* without *Amen.*

b) The psalm *Lauda anima mea* (145) (omitted on the day of death or burial; also omitted on November 2nd).

c) The following verses and responses:

℣. *A porta ínferi.*

℟. *Erue, Dómine, ánimas eórum (ánimam eius).*

℣. *Requiéscant (Requiéscat) in pace.*

℟. *Amen.*

℣. *Dómine, exáudi oratiónem meam.*

℟. *Et clamor meus ad te véniat.*

Orémus.

d) The proper oration chosen from among those found in the Office. If recited for all the faithful departed, the proper prayer is *Fidelium.* On November 2nd, the proper orations are printed in the *Proprium Sanctorum.*

e) The verses and responses:

℣. *Réquiem ætérnam dona eis, Dómine.*

℟. *Et lux perpétua lúceat eis.*

℣. *Requiéscant in pace.*

℟. *Amen.*

} Always in the plural.

118. MATINS

1) The introduction to the Hour of Matins consists of the invitatory with psalm 94 *Venite, exsultemus* recited in the usual way. At its conclusion, instead of the *Glória Patri, Réquiem ætérnam* is said.

2) The Lessons.—There are no absolutions or benedictions for the lessons. The lessons are not concluded with *Tu autem*. All lessons have responses and verses. Therefore there is no *Te Deum*.

3) If Matins is separated from Lauds, the following conclusion is used:

a) The verse and response

℣. *Dómine, exáudi oratiónem meam.*

℟. *Et clamor meus ad te véniat.*

b) The proper oration from among those given after Vespers. It is preceded, as usual, by *Orémus*.

c) The verses and responses

℣. *Réquiem ætérnam dona eis, Dómine.*

℟. *Et lux perpétua lúceat eis.*

℣. *Requiéscant in pace.*

℟. *Amen.*

} Always in the plural.

4) If Lauds is to be omitted entirely, instead of the above conclusion, use the one given after Lauds.

119. Lauds

1) The Hour of Lauds has no introduction. It begins at once with the antiphons and psalms.

2) All the rest is as usual to the *Benedictus* inclusive. However, there is no *capitulum* or hymn.

3) After the *Benedictus* a special conclusion is used. It is the same as the one used at Vespers; but the psalm *Lauda anima* used at Vespers is replaced by the *De profundis*. On the day of death or burial and on November 2nd, the *De profundis* is omitted.

CHAPTER XI

SEASONAL CHANGES

120. We have thus far become familiar with the Office as it is said during the greater part of the year. The fact that it may vary during the various seasons of the ecclesiastical year has already been indicated. For the sake of convenient reference we now list these seasonal changes. There is no need to commit them to memory, as the breviary and Ordo will always note such changes when required.

121. ADVENT

1) The *Te Deum* is said only in festal Offices, but never in the Sunday or ferial Offices.

2) The verse of the *Responsorium breve* of Prime is *Qui ventúrus es in mundum*. This may be replaced only by one proper to a feast on the feast day itself, e.g., by *Qui natus es* on December 8th.

3) In festal Offices the ferial is always commemorated at Lauds and Vespers. The antiphons for the commemorations are found in the *Proprium de Tempore* immediately after the Scripture Occurring lessons for the respective days. The verse and response and the oration are those of the preceding Sunday and are usually reprinted with the antiphons. But note numbers 4 and 5 below.

4) Special antiphons for the *Magnificat*, called "O" antiphons because of their wording, are assigned to each day, beginning with December 17th. If the ferial Office' is not said, these antiphons are used to commemorate the ferial in Vespers on these days.

5) Special antiphons for the *Benedictus* are assigned to December 21st and 23rd. If the ferial Office is not said, they are used to commemorate the ferial at Lauds.

6) In the Sunday Offices the invitatory and the hymns of Matins, Lauds, and Vespers are proper and are found in the *Ordinarium*. The antiphons for Lauds, which are used also in both Vespers and in the Small Hours, as well as all *capitula* and *responsoria brevia*, are given in the *Proprium de Tempore*.

7) In the ferial Office the following points are to be noted: (*a*) The invitatory and hymns of Matins, Lauds, and Vespers are proper and are found in the *Ordinarium*. (*b*) The antiphons for the Small Hours up to December 16th inclusively are those of the Lauds of the preceding Sunday; beginning with the 17th, special antiphons are given in the *Proprium de Tempore* (immediately after the third Sunday of Advent) for Lauds and the Small Hours. (*c*) Special *capitula* and *responsoria brevia* are to be used. They are found in the *Ordinarium*. (*d*) Scheme II of Lauds is always used. (*e*) The *preces* are said on Wednesdays and Fridays at Lauds and Vespers; on Ember Saturday they are said at Lauds.

122. THE NATIVITY SEASON

1) Within the Octave of Christmas.—The Office on days within the octave (on which no feast is celebrated) is *semifestivum* but with a Matins of one nocturn. The

antiphons and psalms are those of Christmas. The lessons are from the *Scriptura occurrens*. A *Gloria Patri* is added to the response after the second lesson. The *Te Deum* concludes the third lesson. At Lauds the antiphons are of the Nativity, the psalms those of Sunday. In the Small Hours the antiphons and psalms are of the current ferial. The rest is from the Nativity. Vespers is the Vespers of the Nativity. The Sunday Compline is said.

2) After the Octave of Christmas. In the ferial Office the antiphons and psalms are from the current ferial. The lessons are from the *Scriptura occurrens*. Add a *Gloria Patri* to the response after the second lesson. The *Te Deum* concludes the third lesson. The *capitula* and *responsoria brevia* are from January 1st for ferial Offices before the 6th of January; from the Epiphany, after January 6th. The oration is either of January 1st or of January 6th until the first Sunday after Epiphany; then it is of the Sunday. The verse in the *responsorium breve* of Prime is *Qui natus es* until January 6th; then it is *Qui apparuísti hódie*.

123. Septuagesima to Passiontide

1) The *alleluia* which concludes the introduction to the various Hours is replaced by the verse *Laus tibi, Christe, Rex œtérnœ glóriœ*. An *alleluia* which is met with anywhere else in the Office is simply dropped.

2) The *Te Deum* is said only in festal Offices; hence not on Sundays.

3) For the Sunday Office special antiphons for the psalms of Lauds are given in the *Proprium de Tempore*.

The antiphons, *capitula, responsoria brevia* for the Small Hours are also found there.

4) In the Sunday and ferial Offices, Scheme II of Lauds is always used.

5) During Lent, feasts of the III class are commemorated only in the ferial Office. On feasts of higher rank the ferial is always commemorated at both Lauds and Vespers.

6) Beginning with Ash Wednesday the following parts are given in the *Proprium de Tempore* for the ferial Office: (*a*) The antiphons for the *Benedictus* and *Magnificat;* (*b*) the prayer for Lauds and the Small Hours; (*c*) a special oration for Vespers.

7) The antiphons, *capitula, responsoria brevia* for the Small Hours of the ferial Office are proper and are given in the *Ordinarium*.

124. PASSIONTIDE

1) In the Sunday and ferial Offices, the *Gloria Patri* is omitted at the end of the Psalm *Venite*, and the invitatory is said twice in full at its conclusion.

2) The *Gloria Patri* is also omitted in all *responsoria brevia* (special ones are given in the *Ordinarium* for the ferial Office) and in the responses after the lessons of Matins.

3) For the first three days of Holy Week, special antiphons are given in the *Proprium de Tempore* for Lauds and the Small Hours.

125. THE LAST THREE DAYS OF HOLY WEEK

NOTE. Those who are present at the liturgical functions on the last three days of Holy Week omit Vespers on Thursday and Friday, Compline on Holy Saturday, and Matins and Lauds on Easter Sunday.

MATINS

1) The whole introduction is omitted. Matins begins with the antiphons and psalms which are proper and are given in the *Proprium de Tempore.*

2) The *Gloria Patri* at the end of the psalms is omitted not only in Matins but in all Hours.

3) The absolution and blessings before the lessons and the *Tu autem* after the lessons are omitted.

LAUDS

1) There is no introduction. The Hour begins with the antiphons and psalms.

2) The antiphons are proper and are given in the *Proprium de Tempore,* but the psalms are of the ferial, Scheme II.

3) The *capitulum* and hymn are omitted, but the verse and response are retained, which are followed, as usual, by the *Benedictus* with its antiphon.

4) After the *Benedictus* a special conclusion is used. It consists of the antiphon *Christus factus est* followed by the *Pater noster* (with *Amen*) and the oration *Réspice* without *Orémus.*

PRIME, TERCE, SEXT, NONE

These hours have no introduction. The Sunday psalms are used but without an antiphon. The conclusion is the one used at Lauds.

VESPERS ON MAUNDY THURSDAY AND GOOD FRIDAY

1) There is no introduction.

2) The antiphons and psalms are proper and are given in the *Proprium de Tempore.*

3) The *capitulum*, hymn, verse and response are omitted; the *Magnificat*, with its antiphon, is retained.

4) After the *Magnificat* the conclusion of Lauds is used.

VESPERS ON HOLY SATURDAY

Vespers on Holy Saturday is like the Vespers on Maundy Thursday except for the following: ·

1) The first antiphon for the psalms is *Hódie;* the others remain unchanged.

2) The antiphon for the *Magnificat* is *Príncipes*.

3) The conclusion consists of the oration *Concéde*. Nothing else is added.

COMPLINE

1) The introduction consists of the *Confiteor* followed by the *Misereatur* and *Indulgentiam*.

2) There is no antiphon for the psalms, which are the psalms of Sunday Compline.

3) After the psalm the *Nunc dimittis* is said, also without an antiphon.

4) The conclusion consists of the antiphon *Christus factus est*, the *Pater noster*, and the usual oration of Compline, *Vísita, quæsumus*. Nothing else is added.

5) On Holy Saturday the antiphon *Christus factus est* is omitted from the conclusion.

126. EASTER AND WITHIN THE OCTAVE

1) All hymns, *capitula*, and *responsoria brevia* are omitted in all Hours. Instead the antiphon *Hæc dies* is said.

2) Matins has only three psalms and three lessons.

3) In Compline the triple *Alleluia* is used as an antiphon after the psalms. The antiphon *Hæc dies* is

said after the *Nunc dimittis*, which is said without its usual antiphon. The rest is as usual.

127. THE PASCHAL SEASON

1) *Alleluia* is added in all Offices to the invitatory, to the antiphons, to all verses and responses, except to the verse in the response after the lessons of Matins, and those given in the *Ordinarium* and printed without *Alleluia*.

2) A double *Alleluia* is added to all *responsoria brevia*.

3) The antiphons for the psalms in the *Psalterium* are not used. Instead of a triple *Alleluia* replaces them except in Matins of the Sunday Office. In a Matins of one nocturn the triple *Alleluia* is said only before the first psalm and after the ninth psalm. Similarly at Lauds and Vespers, the antiphon precedes the first psalm and is repeated only after the last psalm.

4) In the Sunday Office at Matins a special antiphon is used, which is said only before the first psalm and after the last psalm.

5) In Offices of three nocturns, there is usually only one antiphon for each nocturn. It is said before the first psalm and after the third psalm of each nocturn.

6) A special *Commune* is given for Apostles and Evangelists, and another for One or Many Martyrs.

7) The *Te Deum* is said even in ferial Offices.

8) For the Sunday Offices the *capitula* and *responsoria brevia* are proper and are given in the *Proprium de Tempore*.

9) The Litany of the Saints must be added to the Office on St. Mark's day (Major Litanies) after the

Benedicamus Domino of Lauds by those who were not present at the procession during which they were recited. (This is no longer true of the Minor Litanies before the feast of the Ascension.)

128. PENTECOST AND WITHIN THE OCTAVE

Matins has only three psalms and three lessons. The same Office, except for the lessons, is recited each day during the octave. There are no commemorations.

CHAPTER XII

READING THE ORDO

129. Reading the Ordo is a question merely of translating what seems to be a rather cryptic notation. Once the abbreviations given in the beginning of the Ordo have been mastered, little remains to be done. That little can perhaps be done best by a study of examples. The examples are taken from the Roman Ordo for the universal Church for 1961.

FIRST EXAMPLE, FEBRUARY 19.

How printed

19. Viol. DOM. I QUADRAGESIMÆ, De ea, I cl. — Off. dominicale
+ temp. Quadr. — Ad Mat. 9 ant. et 9 pss. de dom. cum versu *Ipse liberavit* (e 1 Nocturno), abs. *Exaudi*, ben. *Ille nos, Divinum auxilium, Per evangelica dicta.* — L.1 (cum suo R.) et 2 (= 2 et 3 cum 3 R.) de Scr. occ., 3 de homilia (= L 7 cum 9 R.), sine *Te Deum.* — Ad LAUDES ant. pr., pss. de dom. (2 loco), rel. pr. — Ad HORAS ant. et rel. pr., ad Primam pss. 53, 118¹, 118², L. brevis *Quærite* (quæ dicitur in omnibus Officiis usque ad sabb. ante dom. I Pass. incl.).

O.C. MISSA pr., sine *Gloria, Credo*, præf. Quadr., *Ite, missa est.* II VESPERAS ut in Psalt. et in pr.

130. This means
February 19th. The color of the vestments is violet. The First Sunday of Lent. The liturgy is of the Sunday, which is a Sunday of the I class. It is a holy day of obligation (that is what the symbol + in the margin

means)—The Office is the Sunday Office for the season of Lent.—At Matins there are 9 antiphons and 9 psalms from the Sunday Psalter. The verse at the conclusion of the psalms is *Ipse liberavit* (from the I Nocturn). The absolution for the lessons is *Exaudi*, the benedictions are *Ille nos, Divinum auxilium, Per evangelica dicta*.—The first lesson (with its response) and the second lesson (which is the former lesson 2 and lesson 3 with the response from lesson 3) are from the Scripture Occurring lessons; lesson three is of the homily (formerly lesson 7 with the response after the 9th lesson); the *Te Deum* is not said.—At Lauds the antiphons are proper and the psalms are taken from Sunday, Scheme II. The rest is proper.—The Small Hours have the antiphon and the rest proper. At Prime the psalms are 53, 118^1, 118^2; the *lectio brevis* is *Quærite* (which is said in all Offices until the Saturday before the first Passion Sunday inclusively).

The Mass is proper, no *Gloria*, but the *Credo* is said, the preface is the preface for Lent. *Ite, missa est* is said. Any oratio imperata is omitted (that is what the marginal O.C. means: omittitur collecta).

Second Vespers is said as given in the *Psalterium* and in the *Proprium de Tempore*.

SECOND EXAMPLE, JUNE 7

How printed

7. Vir. Feria IV, De ea. IV cl. — Off. feriale per annum. — Ad MAT. Ll. de Scr. Occ. cum R.R. e feria IV post dom. IV post Pent., sine Te Deum. — Ad LAUDES or. dom. præc. — ad Primam Cap. *Regi*.
V. MISSA dom. præc., sine *Gloria* et sine *Credo*, præf. comm.,
D. *Ite, missa est*.
   VESPERÆ de feria, or. Dom. præc.

131. This means

June 7. The color of the vestments is green. Wednesday. The liturgy is of the ferial which is a ferial of the IV class.—The Office is the ordinary ferial Office.—At Matins the lessons are the Scripture Occurring lessons with the responses taken from Wednesday after the IV Sunday after Pentecost. The *Te Deum* is not said.—At Lauds the oration is of the preceding Sunday.—At Prime the capitulum is *Regi*.

The Mass is of the preceding Sunday, without *Gloria* or *Credo*. The preface is the common preface. *Ite, missa est* is said.

Vespers is of the ferial. The oration is that of the preceding Sunday.

132. The "V" in the margin means that the votive Masses of the IV class are permitted. The "D" in the margin means that *missæ cotidianæ defunctorum* are permitted.

THIRD EXAMPLE, JULY 14

How printed

> 14. Alb. Feria VI. S. Bonaventuræ E.C.D., III cl.—Off. ordinarium.—L.1 (cum suo R.) et 2 (= 2 et 3 cum 3 R.) de Scr. Occ., 3 de festo (= L. contracta), *Te Deum*.
> MISSA pr., sine *Credo*.
> VESPERÆ de festo.

133. This means

July 14. The color of the vestments is white. Friday. St. Bonaventure, Bishop, Confessor, and Doctor. This is a feast of the III class.—The Office is the ordinary Office.—The first lesson (with its response) and the second lesson (which consists of a combination of lessons 2 and 3 with the response of lesson 3) are from the Scripture Occurring lessons; the third lesson is of the feast (the former contracted lesson). The *Te Deum* is said.

- The Mass is proper and there is no *Credo*.

Vespers is of the feast.

PART II

SPECIMEN OFFICES

NOTE

To learn a science, books are often sufficient; but to acquire an art, in addition to the mastery of the principles, which may be gathered from books, practice is indispensable. The recitation of the Divine Office is an art in more senses than one. Let us therefore consider some typical Offices, and, as far as may be through the medium of cold print, say them together.

CHAPTER XIII

THE OFFICIUM FESTIVUM

134. The Ordo for August 14 reads: I Vesperæ de sequenti Officio festivo proprio. Completorium de dominica. And for August 15: In Assumptione Beatæ Mariæ Virginis. I classis. Officium festivum proprium. Ad Primam in Responsorio brevi Versus erit *Qui natus es.*—II Vesperæ propriæ. Completorium de dominica.

The Office, therefore, of the Feast of the Assumption of the Blessed Virgin Mary begins with First Vespers, and Compline to be said on August 14th.

NOTE 1. In this and the succeeding chapters the various parts of the Office will be quoted from those sections of the breviary where they are properly found. They may, of course, be reprinted in other sections of the breviary in the edition you are using. Thus, many breviaries reprint practically the whole *Ordinarium* in the *Psalterium*, etc. No guide is needed to learn to take advantage of such reprints in convenient places.

NOTE 2. The first words of psalms given in parentheses in the following outlines are to be omitted in the recitation of the Office, because they are identical with the preceding antiphon. (Cf. n. 23.)

135. First Vespers

From the Ordinarium:

℣. + Deus in adjutó-
rium . . .

℞. Dómine, ad adjuván-
dum . . .

Glória Patri. Allelúia.

From the Proprium Sanctorum the antiphons, *from the Commune Festorum B.M.V. per annum* the psalms thus:

Ant. Assúmpta est . . . Dóminum.

Ps. 109. Dixit Dóminus . . .

Glória Patri . . .

Ant. Assúmpta est . . . Dóminum.

Ant. María Virgo . . . sólio.

Ps. 112. Laudáte, servi . . .

Glória Patri . . .

Ant. María Virgo . . . sólio.

Ant. In odórem . . .nimis.

Ps. 121. Lætátus sum . . .

Glória Patri . . .

Ant. In odórem . . . nimis.

Ant. Benedícta . . . communicávimus.

Ps. 126. Nisi Dóminus . . .

Glória Patri . . .

Ant. Benedícta . . . communicávimus.

Ant. Pulchra es . . . ordináta.

Ps. 147. Lauda, Ierúsalem . . .

Glória Patri . . .

Ant. Pulchra es . . . ordináta.

From the Proprium Sanctorum:

Cap. Benedixit te . . . terram. ℞. Deo grátias.

Hymn. O prima, Virgo, . . .

℣. Exaltáta est . . . Génetrix.

℞. Super choros . . . regna.

Ad Magnif. Ant. Virgo . . . ut sol.

From the Ordinarium:

Cant. B.M.V. + Magnificat . . .

Glória Patri . . .

From the Proprium Sanctorum:

Ant. Virgo . . . ut sol.

From the Ordinarium:

℣. Dómine, exáudi . . .

℞. Et clamor meus . . .

Orémus.

From the Proprium Sanctorum:
Oratio. Omnípotens . consórtes.
Per eúndem Dóminum.

From the Ordinarium:
℣. Dómine, exáudi . . .
℟. Et clamor meus . . .
℣. Benedicámus Dómino.
℟. Deo grátias.
℣. Fidélium ánimæ . . .
℟. Amen.

136. COMPLINE

From the Ordinarium:
℣. Iube, Dómine, benedí-cere.
Bened. Noctem quiétam . . . Amen.
Lectio brevis. Fratres: Sóbrii . . . Tu autem . . .
℟. Deo grátias.
℣. + Adiutórium no-strum . . .
℟. Qui fecit cælum . . .
Pater noster. Amen.
Confiteor (omit "et vobis, fratres" and "et vos, fratres":). Misereátur nostri . . . Amen.

+ Indulgéntiam . . . Amen.
℣. + Convérte nos, + Deus . . .
℟. Et avérte iram . . .
℣. + Deus, in adiutó-rium . . .
℟. Dómine, ad adiuván-dum . . .
Glória Patri . . . Allelúia.

From the Psalterium, Dominica ad Comple-torium:
Ant. Miserére mihi meam.
Ps. 4. Cum invocávero . . .
Glória Patri . . .
Ps. 90. Qui degis in . . .
Glória Patri . . .
Ps. 133. Ecce benedí-cite . . .
Glória Patri . . .
Ant. Miserére mihi meam.

From the Ordinarium:
Hymn. Te lucis ante . . .
Cap. Tu autem in nobis . . .
℟. Deo grátias.
℟.br. In manus . . . meum.
In manus . . . meum. Re-demísti . veritátis.
Comméndo . meum.

Glória Patri ... Sancto. In manus ... meum.

℣. Custódi nos ...

℞. Sub umbra alárum ...

Ant. Salva nos in pace.

Cant. Simeonis. + Nunc dimíttis ...

Glória Patri ...

Ant. Salva nos ... in pace.

℣. Dómine, exáudi ...

℞. Et clamor meus ...

Orémus. Vísita, quǽsumus ...

℞. Amen.

℣. Dómine, exáudi ...

℞. Et clamor meus ...

℣. Benedicámus Dómino.

℞. Deo grátias.

Bened. + Benedícat et ...

℞. Amen.

Ant. Fin. B.M.V. Salve, Regína ...

℣. Ora pro nobis ...

℞. Ut digni efficiámur ...

Orémus. Omnípotens sempitérne ...

℞. Amen.

℣. + Divínum auxílium ...

℞. Amen.

137. MATINS

From the Ordinarium:

℣. Dómine, lábia mea ...

℞. Et os meum ...

℣. + Deus, in adiutórium ...

℞. Dómine, ad adjuvándum ...

Glória Patri ... Allelúia.

From the Proprium Sanctorum: the invitatory; *from the Ordinarium the psalm,* 94, Venite, thus:

Invit. Veníte, adorémus ... est cælum. (twice)

Veníte, exsultémus ... ei.

Invit. Veníte, adorémus ... est cælum.

Nam Deus ... ipsius sunt.

Invit. Cuius hódie ... cælum.

Ipsíus est ... manus eius.

Invit. Veníte, adorémus ... assumpta est cælum.

Utinam hódie ópera mea.

Invit. Cuius hódie ... cælum.

Quadragínta annos meam.

Invit. Veníte, adorémus ...
cælum.

Glória Patri ...

Invit. Cuius hódie ... cælum.

Invit. Veníte, adorémus ...
cælum.

*From the Proprium
Sanctorum the hymn.*
Surge! Iam terris ...

The First Nocturn

*From the Proprium
Sanctorum the antiphons,
from the Commune the
psalms.*
Ant. Exaltáta est ...
regna.
Ps. 8. Dómine, Dómine,
noster ...
Glória Patri ...
Ant. Exaltáta est ...
regna.
Ant. Paradísi portæ ...
triúmphas.
Ps. 18. Cæli enárrant ...
Glória Patri ...
Ant. Paradísi portæ ...
triúmphas.

Ant. Benedícta tu ... ven-
tris tui.
Ps. 23. Dómini est terra ...
Glória Patri ...
Ant. Benedícta tu ... ven-
tris tui.
℣. Exaltáta est ...
℟. Super choros ...

From the Ordinarium:
Pater noster (no Amen)
Abs. Exáudi, Dómine, ...
Amen.
℣. Iube, Dómine, bene-
dícere.
Bened. Benedictióne
Amen.

*From the Proprium
Sanctorum:*
Lectio i. De libro Genesis.
Vocavítque Dóminus
ejus.
Tu autem ... Deo grátias.
℟. Vidi speciósam et
thuris. Et sicut ... con-
vállium.

From the Ordinarium:
℣. Iube, Dómine, bene-
dícere.
Bened. Unigénitus
Amen.

From the Proprium Sanctorum:

Lectio ii. De Epístola ... destruétur mors.

Tu autem ... Deo grátias.

℟. Sicut cedrus ... aromatízans. Dedi . . odóris.

From the Ordinarium:

℣. Iube, Dómine, benedícere.

Bened. Spíritus Sancti ...

From the Proprium Sanctorum:

Lectio iii. Opórtet enim ... Iesum Christum.

Tu autem ... Deo grátias.

℟. Quæ est ista ... convállium. Vidérunt eam ... laudavérunt eam. Glória Patri ... Sancto. Vidérunt laudavérunt eam.

The Second Nocturn

From the Proprium Sanctorum the antiphons; *from the Commune* the psalms. *Thus:*

Ant. Spécie tua ... regna.

Ps. 44. Effúndit cor ...

Glória Patri ...

Ant. Spécie tua ... regna.

Ant. Sanctificávit ... Altíssimus.

Ps. 45. Deus est nobis ...

Glória Patri ...

Ant. Sanctificávit ... Altíssimus.

Ant. Gloriósa ... María.

Ps. 86. Fundatiónem suam ...

Glória Patri ...

Ant. Gloriósa ... María.

℣. Assúmpta est ...

℟. Laudántes benedícunt ...

From the Ordinarium:

Pater noster (no Amen.)

Abs. Ipsíus píetas Amen.

℣. Iube, Dómine, benedícere.

Bened. Deus Pater Amen.

From the Proprium Sanctorum:

Lectio iv. Sermo sancti ... núditas.

℣. Tu autem ...

℟. Deo grátias.

℟. Ornátam monílibus... varietáte. Et vidéntes ... tuum.

From the Ordinarium:
℣. Iube, Dómine, bene-dícere.
Bened. Christus perpé-tuæ...

From the Proprium Sanctorum:
Lectio v. Hódie Virgo... assúmitur.
℣. Tu autem...
℟. Deo grátias.
℟. Beátam me ... eum. Quia ... nomen eius.

From the Ordinarium:
℣. Iube, Dómine, bene-dícere.
Bened. Ignem sui...

From the Proprium Sanctorum:
Lectio vi. Ex actis Pii... assúmptam.
℣. Tu autem...
℟. Deo grátias.
℟. Beáta es... Dóminus tecum.

Genuísti ... Virgo. Glória Patri ... Sancto. Genu-ísti... Virgo.

The Third Nocturn

Antiphons *from the Proprium Sanctorum*, psalms *from the Commune.*

Ant. Gaude, María ... mundo.
Ps. 95. Cantáte Dó-mino ...
Glória Patri ...
Ant. Gaude, María ... mundo.
Ant. Cæli annúntiant... eius.
Ps. 96. Dóminus regnat ...
Glória Patri ...
Ant. Cæli annúntiant... eius.
Ant. Cantáte Dómino ... María.
Ps. 97. Cantáte Dó-mino ...
Glória Patri ...
Ant. Cantáte Dómino ... O María.
℣. María Virgo ...
℟. In quo Rex ...

From the Ordinarium:
Pater noster (no Amen)
Abs. A vinculis ... Amen.
℣. Iube, Dómine, bene-
dícere.
Bened. Evangélica léctio
... Amen.

From the Proprium Sanctorum:
Lectio vii. Léctio sancti
Evangélii ... In illo tém-
pore . Et réliqua.
Homília ... potens est.
℣. Tu autem ...
℞. Deo grátias.
℞. Diffúsa est .. tuo.
Proptérea ... ætérnum.

From the Ordinarium:
℣. Iube, Dómine, bene-
dícere.
Bened. Cuius festum ...
Amen.

From the Proprium Sanctorum:
Lectio viii. Quare nos ...
honoráris.
℣. Tu autem ...
℞. Deo grátias.
℞. Beáta es ... Dóminus
tecum.

Intercéde . . nostrum.
Glória Patri ... Sancto.
Intercéde ... nostrum.

From the Ordinarium:
℣. Iube, Dómine, bene-
dícere.
Bened. Ad societátem ...
Amen.

From the Proprium Sanctorum:
Lectio ix. Felix dies ...
habeámus.
℣. Tu autem ... R. Deo
grátias.

From the Ordinarium:
Te Deum laudámus ...

If you stop:
℣. Dómine, exáudi ...
℞. Et clamor meus ...
Orémus.

From the Proprium Sanctorum:
Oratio: Omnípotens ...
consórtes. Per eúndem
Dóminum.

138. LAUDS

From the Ordinarium:
℣. + Deus, in adiutó-
rium ...

℟. Dómine, ad adiuvándum...

Glória Patri ... Allelúia.

The psalms are from the Sunday Psalter, the antiphons from the Proprium Sanctorum: Thus:

Ant. Assúmpta ... Dóminum.

Ps. 92. Dóminus regnat ...

Glória Patri ...

Ant. Assúmpta ... Dóminum.

Ant. María Virgo .. sólio.

Ps. 99. Exsultáte Dómino ...

Glória Patri ...

Ant. María Virgo .. sólio.

Ant. In odórem ... nimis.

Ps. 62. Deus, Deus meus ...

Glória Patri ...

Ant. In odórem ... nimis.

Ant. Benedícta . communicávimus.

Cant. Trium Puer. Benedícite ...

No Glória Patri.

Ant. Benedícta communicávimus.

Ant. Pulchra es ... ordináta.

Ps. 148. Laudáte Dóminum ...

Glória Patri ...

Ant. Pulchra es ... ordináta.

Cap. Benedíxit te ... terram.

℟. Deo grátias.

Hymn. Solis, O Virgo ...

℣. Exaltáta est ...

℟. Super choros ...

Ad Bened. Ant. Quae est ... ordináta?

From the Ordinarium:

Cant. Zach. + Benedíctus ...

From the Proprium Sanctorum:

Ant. Quæ est ... ordináta?

℣. Dómine, exáudi ...

℟. Et clamor meus ...

Orémus. Omnípotens sempitérne . consórtes.

Per eúndem Dóminum.

From the Ordinarium:

℣. Dómine, exáudi ...

℟. Et clamor meus ...

℣. Benedicámus Dómino.
℟. Deo grátias.
℣. Fidélium ánimæ ...
℟. Amen.

139. PRIME

From the Ordinarium:
℣. + Deus, in adiutó-
rium ...
℟. Dómine, ad adiuván-
dum ...
Glória Patri ... Allelúia.
Hymn. Iam lucis orto ...

From the Proprium Sanctorum:
Ant. (L 1.) Assúmpta est
... Dóminum.

From the Sunday Psalter:
Ps. 53. Deus, in nómine ...
Glória Patri ...
Ps. 118^1. Beáti quorum ...
Glória Patri ...
Ps. 118^2. Bene fac ...
Glória Patri ...

From the Proprium Sanctorum:
Ant. Assúmpta est ...
Dóminum.

From the Ordinarium:
Cap. Regi sæculórum ...
Amen.
℟. Deo grátias.
℟. br. Christe ... nobis.
Christe ... nobis. Qui
natus es de María Vír-
gine (The verse is
proper.) Miserére nobis.
Glória Patri ... Sancto.
Christe ... nobis.
℣. Exsúrge, Christe ...
℟. Et líbera nos ...
Orémus. Dómine Deus ...
Amen.
℣. Dómine, exáudi ...
℟. Et clamor meus ...
℣. Benedicámus Dómino.
℟. Deo grátias.
(The Martyrology is read
in choir)
℣. Pretiósa in con-
spéctu ...
℟. Mors sanctórum ejus.
Oratio. Sancta María ...
Amen.
℣. Deus, in adiu- ⎫
tórium ...   ⎬ 3
℟. Dómine, ad adiu- ⎭
vándum ...
Glória Patri ...

Kýrie eléison . . .
Pater noster (no Amen).
℣. Réspice in servos . . .
℟. Et sit splendor . . .
Glória Patri . . .
Orémus. Dirígere et . . .
Amen.
℣. Iube, Dómine, bene-
dícere.
Bened. Dies et actus . . .
Amen.
Lectio brevis. (from the
Sunday Office) Dómi-
nus autem . . .
Tu autem   miserére
nobis.
℟. Deo grátias.
℣. + Adiutórium no-
strum . . .
℟. Qui fecit . . .
℣. Benedícite. ℟. Deus.
Bened. + Dóminus nos
benedícat . . .
℟. Amen.

140. TERCE

From the Ordinarium:
℣. + Deus, in adiutó-
rium . . .

℟. Dómine, ad adiuván-
dum . . .
Glória Patri . . . Allelúia.
Hymn. Nunc, Sancte . . .
Amen.

*Antiphon from the Pro-
prium Sanctorum* (2nd of
L.) *psalms from Sunday.*
Thus:
Ant. María Virgo . . . sólio.
Ps. 118⁸. Osténde mihi . . .
Glória Patri . . .
Ps. 118⁴. Memor esto . . .
Glória Patri . . .
Ps. 118⁵. Bene fecísti . . .
Glória Patri . . .
Ant. María Virgo . . . sólio.

*From the Proprium
Sanctorum:*
Capit. Benedíxit   ter-
ram.
℟. Deo grátias.
℟. br. Exaltáta . . . Géne-
trix. Exaltáta . . . Géne-
trix. Super . . . regna.
Sancta . . . Génetrix.
Glória Patri . . . Sancto.
Exaltáta . . . Génetrix.
℣. Assúmpta est . . .
℟. Laudántes . . .

From the Ordinarium:
℣. Dómine, exáudi . . .
℟. Et clamor meus . . .
Orémus.

From the Proprium Sanctorum:
Oratio. Omnípotens . . . consórtes. Per eúndem Dóminum.

From the Ordinarium:
℣. Dómine, exáudi . . .
℟. Et clamor meus . . .
℣. Benedicámus Dómino.
℟. Deo grátias.
℣. Fidélium ánimæ . . .
℟. Amen.

141. SEXT

From the Ordinarium:
℣. + Deus, in adiutórium . . .
℟. Dómine, ad adiuvándum . . .
Glória Patri . . . Allelúia.
Hymn. Rector potens . . . Amen.

Antiphon from the Proprium Sanctorum (Lauds 3), *psalms from Sunday.* Thus:
Ant. In odórem te nimis.
Ps. 118[6]. Déficit desidério . . .
Glória Patri . . .
Ps. 118[7]. Quam díligo . . .
Glória Patri . . .
Ps. 118[8]. Dúplices corde.
Glória Patri . . .
Ant. In odórem te nimis.

From the Proprium Sanctorum:
Capit. Benedíctus hóminum.
℟. Deo grátias.
℟. br. Assúmpta est . . . Angeli. Assúmpta est . . . Angeli. Laudántes . . . Dóminum. Gaudent Angeli. Glória Patri . . . Sancto. Assúmpta est . . . Angeli.
℣. María Virgo . . . thálamum.
℟. In quo . . . sólio.

From the Ordinarium:
℣. Dómine, exáudi . . .
℟. Et clamor meus . . .
Orémus.

From the Proprium Sanctorum:

Omnípotens sempitérne... consórtes. Per eúndem Dóminum.

From the Ordinarium:

℣. Dómine, exáudi...

℞. Et clamor meus...

℣. Benedicámus Dómino.

℞. Deo grátias.

℣. Fidélium ánimæ...

℞. Amen.

142. NONE

From the Ordinarium:

℣. + Deus, in adiutórium...

℞. Dómine, ad adiuvándum...

Glória Patri... Allelúia.

Hymn. Rerum, Deus,... Amen.

Antiphon from the Proprium Sanct. (Lauds 5) *psalms from Sunday.* Thus:

Ant. Pulchra es... ordináta

Ps. 118⁹. Mirabília sunt...

Glória Patri...

Ps. 118¹⁰. Clamo ex toto...

Glória Patri...

Ps. 118¹¹. Príncipes persequúntur...

Glória Patri...

Ant. Pulchra es... ordináta.

From the Proprium Sanct.:

Cap. Tu glória... nostri.

℞. Deo grátias.

℞. br. María. thálamum. María... thálamum. In quo... sólio. Ad... thálamum. Glória Pátri . . Sancto. María... thálamum.

℣. Dignáre me...

℞. Da mihi...

From the Ordinarium:

℣. Dómine, exáudi...

℞. Et clamor meus...

Orémus.

From the Proprium Sanct.:

Oratio. Omnípotens . consórtes. Per eúndem Dóminum.

From the Ordinarium:

℣. Dómine, exáudi...

℞. Et clamor meus . . .
℣. Benedicámus Dómino.
℞. Deo grátias.
℣. Fidélium ánimæ . . .
℞. Amen.

143. Vespers

From the Ordinarium:
℣. + Deus, in adiutórium . . .
℞. Dómine, ad adiuvándum . . .
Glória Patri . . . Allelúia.

Antiphons from the Proprium, Psalms from the Common. Thus:
Ant. Assúmpta . . . Dóminum.
Ps. 109. Dixit Dóminus . . .
Glória Patri . . .
Ant. Assúmpta . . . Dóminum.
Ant. María Virgo . . . sólio.
Ps. 112. Laudáte, servi . . .
Glória Patri . . .
Ant. María Virgo . . . sólio.
Ant. In odórem . . . nimis.
Ps. 121. Lætátus sum . . .

Glória Patri . . .
Ant. In odórem . . . nimis.
Ant. Benedícta . . com-municávimus.
Ps. 126. Nisi Dóminus . . .
Glória Patri . . .
Ant. Benedícta . . . Com-municávimus.
Ant. Pulchra . . . ordináta.
Ps. 147. Lauda Ierúsalem . . .
Glória Patri . . .
Ant. Pulchra . . . ordináta.
Capit. Benedíxit te . . . terram. ℞. Deo grátias.
Hymn. Ave, maris stella . . .
℣. Exaltáta est . . .
℞. Super choros . . .
Ad Magnif. Ant. Hódie . . . ætérnum.

From the Ordinarium:
Cant. B.M.V. + Magníficat . . .

From the Proprium Sanct.:
Ant. Hódie . . . ætérnum.

From the Ordinarium:
℣. Dómine, exáudi . . .
℞. Et clamor meus . . .
Orémus.

From the Proprium Sanct.:

Omnípotens . . . consórtes.
Per eúndem Dóminum.

From the Ordinarium:

℣. Dómine, exáudi oratiónem . . .

℟. Et clamor meus . . .
℣. Benedicámus Dómino.
℟. Deo grátias.
℣. Fidélium ánimæ . . .
℟. Amen.

COMPLINE is said just as it was after First Vespers.

CHAPTER XIV

THE OFFICIUM DOMINICALE

144. The Ordo for September 9, 10 [1961] reads: I Vesperæ de sequenti dominica ut in Psalterio de Sabbato. Antiphona ad Magnificat *In omnibus*, oratio propria. DOMINICA XVI POST PENTECOSTEN., II Septembris, de ea, II classis. Officium dominicale per annum. Ad Matutinum 9 antiphonæ et 9 psalmi de dominica. Absolutio *Exaudi*, benedictiones *Ille nos, Divinum auxilium, Per evangelica dicta.*—Lectio prima cum suo Responsorio, et lectio secunda (quæ est 2 et 3 cum responsorio de 3) de Scriptura occurrenti, lectio tertia (olim lectio 7) de homilia, *Te Deum.*
Ad II Vesperas ad Magnificat antiphon proprium.
The Office is said as follows.

145. FIRST VESPERS

From the Ordinarium:
℣. + Deus, in adiutórium ...
℟. Dómine, ad adiuvándum ...
Glória Patri ... Allelúia.

From the Psalterium:
Ant. Benedíctus ... meus.
Ps. 143[1]. Benedíctus Dóminus ...
Glória Patri ...
Ant. Benedíctus ... meus.
Ant. Beátus ... eius.

Ps. 143². Deus, cánticum . . .

Glória Patri . . .

Ant. Beátus . . . eius.

Ant. Magnus . . . finis.

Ps. 144¹. Prædicábo te . . .

Glória Patri . . .

Ant. Magnus . . . finis.

Ant. Suávis . . . eius.

Ps. 144². Clemens et . . .

Glória Patri . . .

Ant. Suávis . . . eius.

Ant. Fidélis . . . suis.

Ps. 144⁸. (Fidélis suis.)

Dóminus sústinet . . .

Glória Patri . . .

Ant. Fidélis . . . suis.

Capit. O altitúdo . . . eius!

℟. Deo grátias.

Hymn. Iam sol recédit . . .

℣. Vespertína orátio . . .

℟. Et descéndat super . . .

From the Prop. de Temp.:

Ad Magnif. Ant. In ómnibus . . . locútus est.

From the Ordinarium:

Cant. B.M.V. + Magníficat . . .

From the Prop. de Temp.:

Ant. In ómnibus . . . locútus est.

From the Ordinarium:

℣. Dómine, exáudi oratiónem . . .

℟. Et clamor meus . . .

Orémus.

From the Prop. de Temp.:

Oratio. Tua nos . inténtos. Per Dóminum.

From the Ordinarium:

℣. Dómine, exáudi . . .

℟. Et clamor meus . . .

℣. Benedicámus Dómino.

℟. Deo grátias.

℣. Fidélium ánimæ . . .

℟. Amen.

146. COMPLINE

From the Ordinarium:

℣. Iube, Dómine, benedícere.

Bened. Noctem quiétam . . . Amen.

Lectio br. Fratres: Sóbrii . . .

Tu autem . . . Deo grátias.

℣. + Adiutórium no-
strum . . .

℟. Qui fecit . . .

Pater noster. Amen.

Confíteor. . . .

Misereátur . . .

+ Indulgéntiam . . .

℣. Convérte nos + ...

℟. Et avérte . . .

℣. + Deus, in adiutó-
rium . . .

℟. Dómine, ad adiuván-
dum . . .

Glória Patri . . . Allelúia.

From the Psalterium:

Ant. Intret orátio . . . Dómine.

Ps. 87. Dómine, Deus . . .

Glória Patri . . .

Ps. 102^1. Bénedic, áni-
ma . . .

Glória Patri . . .

Ps. 102^2. Quemádmodum
miserétur . . .

Glória Patri . . .

Ant. Intret orátio . . . Dómine.

From the Ordinarium:

Hymn. Te lucis ante . . .
Amen.

Capit. Tu autem in no-
bis . . .

℟. Deo grátias.

℟.br. In manus . . . meum.

In manus   . meum.

Redemísti . . . Veritátis.

Comméndo . . . meum.

Glória Patri . . . Sancto.

In manus . . . meum.

℣. Custódi nos . . .

℟. Sub umbra . . .

Ant. Salva nos . . . in pace.

Cant. Simeonis. + Nunc
dimíttis . . .

Glória Patri . . .

Ant. Salva nos . . . in pace.

℣. Dómine, exáudi . . .

℟. Et clamor meus . . .

Orémus. Vísita, quǽsu-
mus . . . Per Dóminum.

℣. Dómine, exáudi . . .

℟. Et clamor meus ad . . .

℟.   Benedicámus Dó-
mino.

℟. Deo grátias.

Bened. + Benedícat et
custódiat . . . Amen.

Antiphona B.M.V. Salve,
Regína . . .

℣. Ora pro nobis . . .

℟. Ut digni efficiámur . . .

Orémus. Omnípotens sempitérne ... Per eúndem Christum. Amen.
℣. + Divínum auxílium ...
℞. Amen.

147. MATINS

From the Ordinarium:
℣. Dómine, lábia + mea ...
℞. Et os meum. . . .
℣. + Deus, in adiutórium ...
℞. Dómine, ad adiuvándum ...
Glória Patri ... Allelúia.

The invitatory from the Psalterium, the Venite from the Ordinarium. Thus:
Invit. Dóminum ... adorémus.
Invit. Dóminum ... adorémus.
Ps. 94. Veníte, ... exsultémus ei.
Invit. Dóminum ... adorémus.
Ps. 94. Nam Deus ... sunt.

Invit. Veníte, adorémus.
Ps. 94. Ipsíus est ... eius.
Invit. Dóminum ... adorémus.
Ps. 94. Utinam ... ópera mea.
Invit. Veníte; adorémus.
Ps. 94. Quadragínta . meam.
Invit. Dóminum ... adorémus.
Glória Patri ...
Invit. Veníte, adorémus.
Dóminum ... adorémus.

From the Psalterium:
Hymn. Nocte surgéntes ...
Ant. Beátus vir ... meditátur.
Ps. 1. Beátus vir ...
Glória Patri ...
Ant. Beátus vir ... meditátur.
Ant. Servíte ... tremóre.
Ps. 2. Quare tumultuántur ...
Glória Patri ...
Ant. Servíte ... tremóre.
Ant. Exsúrge Deus meus.
Ps. 3. Dómine, quam ...
Glória Patri ...

Ant. Exsúrge Deus meus.

Ant. Quam admirábile . . . terra.

Ps. 8. Dómine, Dómine noster . . .

Glória Patri . . .

Ant. Quam admirábile . . . terra.

Ant. Sedísti super . . . justítiam.

Ps. 9¹. Celebrábo te . . .

Glória Patri . . .

Ant. Sedísti . . . justítiam.

Ant. Exsúrge . . . homo.

Ps. 9². Psállite Dómino . . .

Glória Patri . . .

Ant. Exsúrge . . . homo.

Ant. Ut quid . . . longe?

Ps. 9³. Quare, Dómine, . .

Glória Patri . . .

Ant. Ut quid . . . longe?

Ant. Exsúrge manus tua.

Ps. 9⁴. Exsúrge, Dómine . . .

Glória Patri . . .

Ant. Exsúrge . . manus tua.

Ant. Iustus . . . diléxit.

Ps. 10. Ad Dóminum . . .

Glória Patri . . .

Ant. Iustus . . . diléxit.

℣. Prævenérunt óculi . . .

℟. Ut meditárer . . .

From the Ordinarium:
Pater noster (no Amen.)

Abs. Exáudi . . . Amen.

℣. Iube, Dómine, benedícere.

Bened. Ille nos. . . . Amen.

From the Prop. de Temp.:
Lectio i. De libro Iob. Et respóndens . . furóre suo.

Tu autem . . . Deo grátias.

℟. Si bona . . . illuc. Dóminus . . . benedíctum.

From the Ordinarium:
℣. Iube, Dómine, benedícere.

Bened. Divínum auxílium . . . Amen.

From the Prop. de Temp.:
Lectio ii. Qui cómmovet . . . sine causa. Tu autem . . . Deo grátias.

℟. Quare detraxístis . iniquitátem. Verúmta-

men ... expléte. Glória
Patri   Sancto. Ve-
rúmtamen ... expléte.

From the Ordinarium:
℣. Iube, Dómine, benedí-
-cere.
Bened. Ad societátem ...
Amen.

*From the Prop. de
Temp.:*
Lectio iii. Léctio S. Evang.
... In illo tempore ... et
réliqua.   Homília
avarítiæ est. Tu autem
... Deo grátias.

From the Ordinarium:
Te Deum ...

If you stop.
℣. Dómine, exáudi ...
℞. Et clamor meus ...
Orémus.

*From the Prop. de
Temp.:*
Oratio. Tua nos, .   in-
téntos. Per Dóminum.

From the Ordinarium:
℣. Dómine, exáudi ...
℞. Et clamor meus ...
℣. Benedicámus Dómino.
℞. Deo grátias.

℣. Fidélium ánimæ ...
℞. Amen.

148. LAUDS

From the Ordinarium:
℣. + Deus, in adiutó-
rium ...
℞. Dómine, ad adiuván-
dum ...
Glória Patri ... Allelúia.

From the Psalterium:
Ant. Allelúia Dóminus ...
Allelúia.
Ps. 92. Dóminus regnat ...
Glória Patri ...
Ant. Allelúia Dóminus ...
Allelúia.
Ant. Iubiláte ... allelúia.
Ps. 99. Exsultáte Dó-
mino ...
Glória Patri ...
Ant. Iubiláte .   . allelúia.
Ant. Benedícam ... alle-
lúia.
Ps. 62. Deus, Deus
meus ...
Glória Patri ...
Ant. Benedícam ... alle-
lúia.
Ant. Tres púeri ... alle-
lúia.

Cant. Benedícite, ómnia ...
No Glória Patri.
Ant. Tres puéri ... allelúia.
Ant. Allelúia, laudáte ...
allelúia.
Ps. 148. Laudáte Dómi-
num ...
Glória Patri ...
Ant. Allelúia, laudáte ...
allelúia.
Capit. Benedíctio   .
Amen.
℞. Deo grátias.
Hymn. Ecce iam noctis ...
℣. Dóminus regnávit ...
℞. Induit Dóminus ...

*Antiphon from the Pro-
prium, Benedictus from the
Ordinarium:*
Ant. Cum intráret ... di-
mísit.
Cant. + Benedíctus Dó-
minus ...
Glória Patri ...
Ant. Cum intráret ... di-
mísit.

From the Ordinarium:
℣. Dómine, exáudi ...
℞. Et clamor meus ...
Orémus.

*From the Proprium de
Temp.:*
Oratio. Tua nos, . . in-
téntos. Per Dóminum.

From the Ordinarium:
℣. Dómine, exáudi ...
℞. Et clamor meus ...
℣. Benedicámus Dómino.
℞. Deo grátias.
℣. Fidélium ánimæ ...
℞. Amen.

149. PRIME

From the Ordinarium:
℣. + Deus, in adiutó-
rium ...
℞. Dómine, ad adiuván-
dum ...
Glória Patri ... allelúia.
Hymn. Iam lucis orto ...

From the Psalterium:
Ant. Allelúia, confitémini
... allelúia.
Ps. 117. Grátias ágite ...
Glória Patri ...
Ps. 118^1. Beáti quorum ...
Glória Patri ...
Ps. 118^2. Bene fac servo ...
Glória Patri ...

Ant. Allelúia, confitémini
... allelúia.

From the Ordinarium:
Capit. Regi sæculórum ...
. Amen.
℞. Deo grátias.
℞.br. Christe nobis.
Christe . nobis. Qui
sedes . . Patris. Mise-
rére nobis. Glória Patri
... Sancto. Christe ...
nobis.
℣. Exsúrge ...
℞. Et líbera ...
℣. Dómine, exáudi ...
℞. Et clamor meus ...
Orémus. Dómine Deus ...
Per Dóminum.
℣. Dómine, exáudi ...
℞. Et clamor meus ...
℣. Benedicámus Dómino.
℞. Deo grátias.
℣. Pretiósa in con-
spéctu ...
Oratio. Sancta María ...
Amen.
℣. Deus, in adiutó-
rium ...
℞. Dómine, ad ad-
iuvándum ...   } 3

Glória Patri Sicut
erat ...
Kýrie eléison ...
Pater noster (no Amen).
℣. Réspice in servos ...
℞. Et sit splendor ...
℣. Glória Patri ...
℞. Sicut erat ...
Orémus. Dirígere et ...
Amen.
℣. Iube, Dómine, benedí-
cere.
Bened. Dies et actus ...
Amen.
Lect. br. Dóminus au-
tem ...
Tu autem. ...
℞. Deo grátias.
℣. + Adiutórium no-
strum ...
℞. Qui fecit cælum ...
℣. Benedícite. R. Deus.
Bened. + Dóminus nos
benedícat ... Amen.

150. TERCE

From the Ordinarium:
℣. + Deus, in adiutó-
rium ...
℞. Dómine, ad adiuván-
dum ...

Glória Patri . . . Allelúia.
Hymn. Nunc, Sancte, nobis . . .

From the Psalterium:
Ant. Allelúia . . . allelúia.
Ps. 118³. Osténde mihi, . . .
Glória Patri . . .
Ps. 118⁴. Memor esto . . .
Glória Patri . . .
Ps. 118⁵. Bene fecísti . . .
Glória Patri . . .
Ant. Allelúia, deduc . . . Allelúia.
Capit. Deus cáritas . . . in eo.
℟. Deo grátias.
℟.br. Inclína . . . tua. Inclína . . . tua. Avérte . . . me. In . . . tua. Glória Patri . . . Sancto. Inclína . . . tua.
℣. Ego dixi . . .
℟. Sana ánimam . . .

From the Ordinarium but the oration from the Proprium:
℣. Dómine, exáudi . . .
℟. Et clamor meus . . .
Orémus. Tua nos, . . . inténtos. Per Dóminum.
℣. Dómine, exáudi . . .

℟. Et clamor meus . . .
℣. Benedicámus Dómino.
℟. Deo grátias.
℣. Fidélium ánimæ
Amen.

151. SEXT

From the Ordinarium:
℣. + Deus, in adiutórium . . .
℟. Dómine, ad adiuvándum . . .
Glória Patri . . . Allelúia.
Hymn. Rector potens . . .
Amen.

From the Psalterium:
Ant. Allelúia, tuus . . . allelúia.
Ps. 118⁶. Déficit desidério . . .
Glória Patri . . .
Ps. 118⁷. Quam díligo . . .
Glória Patri . . .
Ps. 118⁸. Dúplices corde . . .
Glória Patri . . .
Ant. Allelúia, tuus . . . allelúia.
Capit. Alter altérius . . .
℟. Deo grátias.

℞.br. In ... tuum. In ...
tuum. In sæculum .
tụa. Pérmanet ... tuum.
Glória Patri ... Sancto.
In ætérnum ... tuum.
℣. Dóminus regit ...
℞. In loco páscuæ ...

*From the Ordinarium
but the oration from the
Proprium:*
℣. Dómine, exáudi ...
℞. Et clamor meus ...
Orémus. Tua nos, ... in-
téntos. Per Dóminum.
℣. Dómine, exáudi ...
℞. Et clamor meus ...
℣. Benedicámus Dómino.
℞. Deo grátias.
℣. Fidélium ánimæ. ...
Amen.

152. NONE

From the Ordinarium:
℣. + Deus, in adiutó-
rium ...
℞. Dómine, ad adiuván-
dum ...
Glória Patri ... Allelúia.
Hymn. Rerum, Deus ...
Amen.

From the Psalterium:
Ant. Allelúia, faciem ...
allelúia.
Ps. 118⁹. Mirabília sunt ...
Glória Patri ...
Ps. 118¹⁰. Clamo ex toto ...
Glória Patri ...
Ps. 118¹¹. Príncipes ...
Glória Patri ...
Ant. Allelúia, faciem
Allelúia.
Capit. Empti enim ... ve-
stro.
℞. Deo grátias.
℞.br. Clamávi ... Dómi-
ne. Clamávi ... Domine.
Justificatiónes tuas re-
quíram. Exáudi ... Dó-
mine. Glória Patri ...
Sancto. Clamávi ... Dó-
mine.
℣. Ab occúltis ...
℞. Et ab aliénis ...

*From the Ordinarium
but the oration from the
Proprium:*
℣. Dómine, exáudi ...
℞. Et clamor meus ...
Orémus. Tua nos . . in-
téntos. Per Dóminum.
℣. Dómine, exáudi ...

℟. Et clamor meus...

℣. Benedicámus Dómino.

℟. Deo grátias.

℣. Fidélium ánimæ
Amen.

153. VESPERS

From the Ordinarium:

℣. + Deus, in adiutórium...

℟. Dómine, ad adiuvándum...

Glória Patri... Allelúia.

From the Psalterium:

Ant. Dixit Dóminus
meis.

Ps. 109. (Dixit ... meis),
donec...

Glória Patri...

Ant. Dixit Dóminus ...
meis.

Ant. Magna ... eius.

Ps. 110. Celebrábo Dóminum...

Glória Patri...

Ant. Magna ... eius.

Ant. Qui timet ... nimis.

Ps. 111. Beátus vir ...

Glória Patri...

Ant. Qui timet ... nimis.

Ant. Sit nomen ... sǽcula.

Ps. 112. Laudáte, servi ...

Glória Patri...

Ant. Sit nomen ... sǽcula.

Ant. Deus autem ... fecit.

Ps. 113. Cum exíret ...

Glória Patri...

Ant. Deus autem ... fecit.

Capit. Benedíctus ... nostra.

℟. Deo grátias.

Hymn. Lucis Creator
Amen.

℣. Dirigátur, Dómine, ...

℟. Sicut incénsum ...

The antiphon from the Proprium, the Magnificat from the Ordinarium:

Ant. ad Magnif. Cum vocátus ... Allelúia.

Cant. B.M.V. + Magníficat ...

Glória Patri...

Ant. Cum vocátus ... allelúia.

From the Ordinarium, but the oration from the Proprium:

℣. Dómine, exáudi ...

℞. Et clamor meus . . .
Orémus. Tua nos, . . . inténtos. Per Dóminum.
℣. Dómine, exáudi . . .
℞. Et clamor meus . . .
℣. Benedicámus Dómino.
℞. Deo grátias.

℣. Fidélium ánimæ . .
Amen.

COMPLINE is said just as it was after First Vespers of an *Officium festivum*. See paragraph 136.

CHAPTER XV

THE OFFICIUM ORDINARIUM

154. The Ordo for November 10, 1961, reads:
Feria VI, S. Andreæ Avellini Confessoris, III classis.—
Officium ordinarium.—Lectio prima (cum suo responsorio) et lectio secunda (quæ est 2 et 3 cum responsorio 3) de Scriptura occurrenti, lectio tertia de festo (et est lectio contracta), *Te Deum.*—Ad Laudes commemoratio Ss. Tryphonis et Sociorum, Martyrum. —Vesperæ de festo, sine commemoratione.

The Office will be said as follows:

155. MATINS

From the Ordinarium:

℣. Dómine, lábia + mea . . .

℟. Et os meum . . .

℣. + Deus, in adiutórium . . .

℟. Dómine, ad adiuvándum . . .

Glória Patri . . . Allelúia.

Invit. et hymn. de Communi Conf. Non Pont., Ps. 94 de Ord.

Invit. Regem . . . adorémus.

Invit. Regem adorémus.

Ps. 94. Veníte . . . ei.

Invit. Regem . adorémus.

Ps. 94. Nam Deus . . . sunt.

Invit. Veníte, adorémus.

Ps. 94. Ipsíus . . . eius.

Invit. Regem . . . adorémus.

Ps. 94. Utinam . . . ópera mea.

Invit. Venite, adorémus.

Ps. 94. Quadragínta . . . meam.

Invit. Regem . . adorémus.

Glória Patri . . .

Invit. Veníte, adorémus.

Invit. Regem . . adorémus.

Hymn. Iste conféssor . . . Amen.

From the Psalterium (F. VI)

Ant. Suscitávit . . . Israel.

Ps. 77¹. Auscúlta, pópule . . .

Glória Patri . . .

Ant. Suscitávit . . . Israel.

Ant. Coram . . . mirabília.

Ps. 77². Fílii Ephraim . . .

Glória Patri . . .

Ant. Coram . . . mirabília.

Ant. Iánuas . manducándum.

Ps. 77³. Sed perrexérunt . . .

Glória Patri . . .

Ant. Iánuas manducándum.

Ant. Deus adiútor . . . est.

Ps. 77⁴. Sed támen peccavérunt: . . .

Glória Patri . . .

Ant. Deus adiútor . . . est.

Ant. Redémit . . . tribulántis.

Ps. 77⁵. Quóties provocavérunt . . .

Glória Patri . . .

Ant. Redémit . . . tribulántis.

Ps. 77⁶. Sed tentavérunt . . .

Glória Patri . . .

Ant. Ædificávit . . . terra.

Ant. Adjuva nos . . . nostris.

Ps. 78. Deus, venérunt . . .

Glória Patri . . .

Ant. Adjuva nos . . . nostris.

Ant. Ego sum . . . Ægýpti.

Ps. 80. Exsultáte Deo . . .

Glória Patri . . .

Ant. Ego sum . . . Ægýpti.

Ant. Ne táceas . . . caput.

Ps. 82. Noli, Dómine . . .
Glória Patri . . .
Ant. Ne táceas . . . caput.
℣. Cognóscant quia . . .
℟. Tu solus Altíssimus . . .

From the Ordinarium:
Pater noster (no Amen.)
Abs. Ipsíus píetas .
Amen.
℣. Iube, Dómine, bene-
dícere.
Bened. Ille nos . . . Amen.

*From the Prop. de
Temp.:* (For the 1st week
of November)
Lectio I De Ezechiéle
Prophéta
Et factus est . . . óperis. Tu
autem . . . Deo grátias.
℟. Super muros . . . meam.
Tota die . . . Dómini.

From the Ordinarium:
℣. Iube, Dómine, bene-
dícere.
Bened. Cuius festum . . .
Amen.

*From the Prop. de
Temp.:*
Lectio II. Proptérea .
Deus. Et factus est . . .

nata es. Tu autem . . .
Deo grátias. ℟. Susti-
núimus . . . tuam. Non ,
in . . . nos. Glória Patri
. . . Sancto. Non in . . .
nos.

From the Ordinarium:
℣. Iube, Dómine, bene-
dícere.
Bened. Ad societátem . . .
Amen.

From the Prop. Sanct.:
Lectio III. Andréas Avellí-
nus . exspirávit. Tu
autem . . . Deo grátias.

From the Ordinarium:
Te Deum laudámus . . .

If you stop:
℣. Dómine, exáudi . . .
℟. Et clamor meus . . .
Orémus.

From the Prop. Sanct.:
Deus, qui in corde . . . perducámur. Per Dómi-
num.

From the Ordinarium:
℣. Dómine, exáudi. . .
℟. Et clamor meus . . .
℣. Benedicámus Dómino.

℟. Deo gratias.
℣. Fidélium ánimæ . . .
℟. Amen.

156. LAUDS

From the Ordinarium:
℣. + Deus, in adiutó-
rium . . .
℟. Dómine, ad adiuván-
dum . . .
Glória Patri . . . Alleluia.

From the Psalterium:
Ant. Exaltáte . . . eius.
Ps. 98. Dóminus regnat . . .
Glória Patri . . .
Ant. Exaltáte . . . eius.
Ant. Eripe me . . . confúgi.
Ps. 142. Dómine, audi . . .
Glória Patri . . .
Ant. Eripe me . . . confúgi.
Ant. Benedixísti . . . tuæ.
Ps. 84. Propítius fuísti. . . .
Glória Patri . . .
Ant. Benedixísti . . . tuæ.
Ant. In Dómino . . . Israel.
Cant. Isaiæ. Vere tu es . . .
Glória Patri . . .
Ant. In Dómino . . . Israel.
Ant. Lauda . . . Dóminum.
Ps. 147. (Lauda . . . Domi-
num) lauda Deum . . .

Glória Patri . . .
Ant. Lauda . . . Dóminum.

*From the Com. Conf.
non Pont.:*
Capit. Beátus vir . . . vita
sua.
℟. Deo grátias.
Hymn. Iesu, coróna . . .
Amen.
℣. Iustum dedúxit . . .
℟. Et osténdit . . .
Ad Bened. Ant. Euge,
serve . . . Dómini tui.

From the Ordinarium:
Cant. Zach. + Benedíctus
Dóminus . . .
Glória Patri . . .

From the Com. Sanct.:
Ant. Euge, serve . . . tui.

From the Ordinarium:
℣. Dómine, exáudi . . .
℟. Et clamor meus . . .
Orémus.

From the Prop. Sanct.:
Deus, qui in . . . perducámur. Per Dóminum.

*From the Commune
Virg. or Prop. Sanct.:*
Ant. Vestri capílli . . . vos.
℣. Exsultábunt Sancti . . .

℞. Lætabúntur in . . .

Orémus. Fac nos, quǽsumus . . . sentiámus. Per Dóminum.

From the Ordinarium:

℣. Dómine, exáudi . . .

℞. Et clamor meus . . .

℣. Benedicámus Dómino.

℞. Deo grátias.

℣. Fidélium ánimæ. . . .

℞. Amen.

157. PRIME

From the Ordinarium:

℣. + Deus, in adiutórium . . .

℞. Dómine, ad adiuvándum . . .

Glória Patri . . . Allelúia.

Hymn. Iam lucis orto . . .

From the Psalterium:

Ant. Ne discédas . . ádiuvet.

Ps. 21¹. Deus meus, . . .

Glória Patri . . .

Ps. 21². Circúmstant me . . .

Glória Patri . . .

Ps. 21³. Enarrábo nomen . . .

Glória Patri . . .

Ant. Ne discédas . . . adiuvet.

From the Ordinarium:

Capit. Regi sæculórum . . .

℞. Deo grátias.

℞. br. Christe . . nobis. Christe . . . nobis. Qui sedes . . . Patris. Miserére nobis. Glória Patri . . . Sancto. Christe . . . nobis.

℣. Exsúrge, Christe . . .

℞. Et líbera nos . . .

℣. Dómine, exáudi . . .

℞. Et clamor meus . . .

Orémus. Dómine Deus . . . Per Dóminum.

℣. Dómine, exáudi . . .

℞. Et clamor meus . . .

℣. Benedicámus Dómino.

℞. Deo grátias.

℣. Pretiósa in . . .

℞. Mors Sanctórum ejus.

Sancta María . . . Sæculórum.

℞. Amen.

℣. Deus, in adiutórium . . .

℞. Dómine, ad adiuvándum . . .

} 3

Glória Patri Sicut
erat . . .
Kýrie eléison, . . .
Pater noster (no
Amen.)
℣. Réspice in servos . . .
℟. Et sit splendor . . .
Glória Patri Sicut
erat . . .
Orémus. Dirígere et . .
Amen.
℣. Iube, Dómine, bene-
dícere.
Bened. Dies et actus . . .
Amen.
Lectio br. Dóminus
autem . . .
Tu autem . . . Deo grátias.
℣. + Adjutórium no-
strum . . .
℟. Qui fecit cælum . . .
℣. Benedícite. ℟. Deus.
Bened. + Dóminus nos
benedícat . . . Amen.

158. TERCE

From the Ordinarium:
℣ + Deus, in adiu-
tórium . . .
℟. Dómine, ad adiuván-
dum . . .

Glória Patri . . . Allelúia.
Hymn. Nunc, Sancte, . . .
Amen.

From the Psalterium:
Ant. Excita . . . fácias nos.
Ps. 79¹. Qui pascis . . .
Glória Patri . . .
Ps. 79². Vitem ex
Ægýpto . . .
Glória Patri . . .
Ps. 81. Deus assúrgit in . . .
Glória Patri . . .
Ant. Excita . . . Fácias nos.

*From the Commune
Sanctorum:*
Capit. Beátus vir, . . . sua.
℟. Deo grátias.
℟. br. Amávit . . eum.
Amávit . . . eum. Stolam
. . . eum. Et . . . eum.
Glória Patri . . . Sancto.
Amávit . . . eum.
℣. Os justi . . .
℟. Et lingua . . .

*From the Ord. but the
prayer from the Proprium:*
℣. Dómine, exáudi . . .
℟. Et clamor meus . . .
Orémus. Deus, qui in . . .
perducámur. Per Dómi-
num.

℣. Dómine, exáudi ...
℞. Et clamor meus ...
℣. Benedicámus Dómino.
℞. Deo grátias.
℣. Fidélium ánimæ .
Amen.

159. SEXT

From the Ordinarium:
℣ + Deus, in adjutó-
rium ...
℞. Dómine, ad adjuván-
dum ...
Glória Patri ... Alleluia.
Hymn. Rector potens, ...
Amen.

From the Psalterium:
Ant. Beáti qui ... Dómine.
Ps. 83¹. Quam dilécta ...
Glória Patri ...
Ps. 83². Dómine exercí-
tuum ...
Glória Patri ...
Ps. 86. Fundatiónem
suam ...
Glória Patri ...
Ant. Beáti qui ... Dómine.

*From the Commune
Sanct.:*
Capit. Iustus cor ... depre-
cábitur.

℞. Deo grátias.
℞. br. Os ... sapiéntiam.
Os sapiéntiam. Et
lingua . iudícium.
Meditábitur sapiéntiam.
Glória Patri ... Sancto.
Os ... sapiéntiam.
℣. Lex Dei ejus ...
℞. Et non supplantabún-
tur ...

*From the Ordinarium
but the oration from the
Proprium:*
℣. Dómine, exáudi ...
℞. Et clamor meus ...
Orémus. Deus, qui in
corde . . perducámur.
Per Dóminum.
℣. Dómine, exáudi ...
℞. Et clamor meus ...
℣. Benedicámus Dómino.
℞. Deo grátias.
℣. Fidélium ánimæ
Amen.

160. NONE

From the Ordinarium:
℣. + Deus, in adiutó-
rium ...
℞. Dómine, ad adiuván-
dum ...

Glória Patri ... Alleluia.

Hymn. Rerum, Deus, ...
Amen.

From the Psalterium:
Ant. Misericórdia ... Dómine.

Ps. 88¹. Grátias Dómini ...
Glória Patri ...
Ps. 88². Olim locútus es ...
Glória Patri ...
Ps. 88⁸. Tu vero ...
Glória Patri ...
Ant. Misericórdia ... Dómine.

From the Commune Sanct.:
Capit. Iustum dedúxit ...
℞. Deo grátias.
℞. br. Lex ... ipsíus. Lex
. ipsíus. Et non . .
eius. In ipsíus.
Glória Patri ... Sancto.
Lex ... ipsíus.
℣. Iustum dedúxit ...
℞. Et osténdit ...

From the Ordinarium,
but the oration from the
Proprium:
℣. Dómine, exáudi ...
℞. Et clamor meus ...

Orémus. Deus, qui in ...
perducámur. Per Dóminum.
℣. Dómine, exáudi ...
℞. Et clamor meus ...
℣. Benedicámus Dómino.
℞. Deo grátias.
℣. Fidélium ánimæ
Amen.

161. VESPERS
From the Ordinarium:
℣. + Deus, in adiutórium ...
℞. Dómine, ad adiuvándum ...
Glória Patri ... Allelúia.
From the Psalterium:
Ant. Dómine cognovísti me.
Ps. 138¹. Dómine, scrutáris ...
Glória Patri ...
Ant. Dómine cognovísti me.
Ant. Mirabília ... nimis.
Ps. 138². Tu enim formásti ...
Glória Patri ...
Ant. Mirabília ... nimis.
Ant. Ne derelínquas
meæ.

Ps. 139. Eripe me, Dó-
mine ...

Glória Patri ...

Ant. Ne derelínquas . .
meæ.

Ant. Dómine, . . exáudi
me.

Ps. 140. Dómine,
clamo ...

Glória Patri ...

Ant. Dómine, . . exáudi
me.

Ant. Educ de ... tuo.

Ps. 141. Voce magna
ad ...

Glória Patri ...

Ant. Educ de ... tuo.

From the Commune:

Capit. Beátus vir, ... sua.

℟. Deo grátias.

Hymn. Iste Conféssor ...
Amen.

℣. Iustum dedúxit...

℟. Et osténdit ...

Ad Magnif. Ant. Hic vir
... manu.

From the Ordinarium:

Cant. B.M.V. + Magnifi-
cat ...

Glória Patri ...

From the Commune:

Ant. Hic vir ... manu.

*From the Ordinarium
but the oration from the
Proprium:*

℣. Dómine, exáudi ...

℟. Et clamor meus ...

Orémus. Deus, qui in ...
perducámur. Per Dómi-
num.

℣. Dómine, exáudi ...

℟. Et clamor meus ...

℣. Benedicámus Dómino.

℟. Deo grátias.

℣. Fidélium ánimæ
Amen.

162. COMPLINE

From the Ordinarium:

℣. Iube, Dómine, bene-
dícere.

Bened. Noctem quiétam
... Amen.

Lectio br. Fratres:
sóbrii ...

Tu autem ... Deo grátias.

℣. + Adiutórium no-
strum ...

℟. Qui fecit ...

Pater noster ... Amen.

Confíteor. Misereá-
tur ...

+ Indulgéntiam ...

℣. Convérte nos, +
Deus ...

℞. Et avérte iram ...

℣. + Deus, in adiutó-
rium ...

℞. Dómine, ad adiuván-
dum ...

Glória Patri ... Allelúia.

From the Psalterium:

Ant. Voce mea ... Deus.

Ps. 76¹. Vox mea ad ...

Glória Patri ...

Ps. 76². Deus, sancta
est ...

Glória Patri ...

Ps. 85. Inclína, Dó-
mine, ...

Glória Patri ...

Ant. Voce mea ... Deus.

From the Ordinarium:

Hymn. Te lucis ante ...
Amen.

Capit. Tu autem in
noster.

℞. Deo grátias.

℞. br. In manus ... meum.
In manus ... meum. Re-
demísti . veritátis.
Comméndo . meum.

Glória Patri ... Sancto.
In manus ... meum.

℣. Custódi nos ...

℞. Sub umbra ...

Ant. Salva nos ... in pace.

Cant. Simeonis. + Nunc
dimíttis ...

Glória Patri ...

Ant. Salva nos ... in pace.

℣. Dómine, exáudi ...

℞. Et clamor meus ...

Orémus. Vísita, quǽsu-
mus ...

Per Dóminum.

℣. Dómine, exáudi ...

℞. Et clamor meus ...

℣. Benedicámus Dómino.

℞. Deo grátias.

Bened. + Benedícat et ...

℞. Amen.

Antiphona B.M.V.

Salve, Regína, mater ...

℣. Ora pro nobis ...

℞. Ut digni ...

Orémus. Omnípotens, sem-
pitérne Deus, Per
eúmdem Christum Dó-
minum nostrum.

℞. Amen.

℣. + Divínum auxí-
lium ...

℞. Amen.

INDEX

References are to paragraph numbers

117

Made in the USA
Middletown, DE
04 March 2021